BLUE RIDGE NATURE JOURNAL

Geographic Provinces of the Southern Appalachian Region

1 = Appalachian Plateau
2 = Ridge and Valley
3 = Blue Ridge
4 = Piedmont

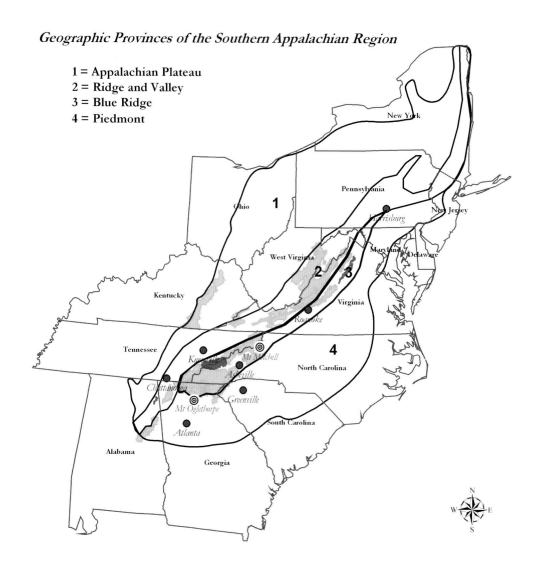

BLUE RIDGE NATURE JOURNAL

REFLECTIONS ON THE APPALACHIAN MOUNTAINS
IN ESSAYS AND ART

essays by

GEORGE ELLISON

with paintings by

ELIZABETH ELLISON

natural

HISTORY
PRESS

Published by Natural History Press
A Division of The History Press
Charleston, SC 29403
www.historypress.net

Copyright © 2006 by George and Elizabeth Ellison
All rights reserved

Cover Image: The Master Gardener, watercolor, 24 x 18 inches
Frontispiece: Map by Matt Roark

First published 2006

Manufactured in the United Kingdom

ISBN 1.59629.139.7

Library of Congress Cataloging-in-Publication Data

Ellison, George, 1941-
  Blue Ridge nature journal : reflections on the Appalachian Mountains
in essays and art / George and Elizabeth Ellison.
    p. cm.
  ISBN 1-59629-139-7 (alk. paper)
  1. Natural history--Appalachian Mountains. I. Ellison, Elizabeth. II.
Title.
  QH104.5.A6.E45 2006
  508.755--dc22
                  2006016740

FOR NELLIE WIGGINS

who

MADE A LOT OF THINGS POSSIBLE

HERE IN THE MOUNTAINS

CONTENTS

Preface   9

I. THE BLUE RIDGE PROVINCE: AN OVERVIEW   11

II. FLORA
  1. The Yellow Birch and Boulder Syndrome   22
  2. Table Mountain Pine: Arboreal Emblem   24
  3. Black Gum: Rabbit Traps and Bee Gums   26
  4. Sourwood: Natural Bends and Sled Runners   29
  5. *Sarvis*: What's in a Name?   31
  6. Azaleas and Rhododendrons   33
  7. Highland Doghobble: The Black Bear's Refuge   36
  8. Galax: Odiferous and Decorative   38
  9. Oil Nut: That Most Curious Fruit   40
  10. Hepatica: "The Gem of the Woods"   42
  11. The Spring Ephemeral Strategy   44
  12. Plant Traps: By Devious Means   47
  13. Cherokee Baskets: Splints and Dyes   50
  14. Winter Orchids: Puttyroot and Cranefly Orchis   53
  15. Fiddleheads and Ferns That Walk   55
  16. Cherokee Mushrooms: Slicks, Milkys and Wishys   57
  17. White Snakeroot: The Milk Sick Story   59

III. Fauna

1. Bird Lore 64
2. Wolf Lore 67
3. Panther Lore 70
4. Bear Lore 73
5. Fox Lore 75
6. Raccoon Lore 77
7. Skunks: Striped and Spotted 79
8. Mountain Boomers: "Our Speediest Varmint" 81
9. Honeybee Lore 83
10. Cherokee Cookery: Yellow Jacket Soup and More 85
11. *Tlanuwas* and *Uktenas* 87
12. Copperheads and Timber Rattlers 89

IV. Paintings

IV. Paintings 93

Artwork Specifications 140
Sources 141
About the Author and Artist 144

PREFACE

S ince we moved with our three children to western North Carolina in 1973, Elizabeth and I have been enchanted with the region's landscapes, plants and animals. As a part of our continuous exploration of these mountains, we have tried to capture in words and paint the things—both large and small—we have discovered, as well as our feelings about them. We are thrilled by the opportunity this book affords us to share with others some of these perspectives, images and feelings.

The materials have been gathered into four broad sections: an overview of the geologic origins and present-day geographic setting of the Blue Ridge Province, two gatherings of essays that focus respectively on various aspects of the region's flora and fauna and a section devoted to Elizabeth's full-color paintings in which she records her observations. I've chosen subject matter that, for the most part, hasn't appeared time and again in other natural history books about the region. Accordingly, I've omitted topics such as ramps (the famous and edible wild onion), Fraser fir (the high-country conifer found only in the Blue Ridge), shortia (the so-called "lost plant of Appalachia"), the demise of the American chestnut, the multitude of salamander species and others.

Since the common names of plants vary from person to person and region to region, I have, where appropriate, provided scientific names. This nomenclature is based upon the names used at the University of Tennessee Herbarium, whose website is maintained by B. Eugene Wofford, the herbarium's curator.

People—especially the ancient Cherokees, early white settlers and their descendants—are an important part of the natural history of the Blue Ridge. Throughout, I have incorporated many of their observations as well as their lore and humor.

The essays originally appeared in three publications. My "Nature Journal" column for the *Asheville Citizen-Times* started appearing, along with Elizabeth's illustrations, in 1988. Through the years, numerous editors have assisted us with texts and images at every turn. We particularly want to thank Bill Moore, Jim Crawford, Ned Jennings, Lydia Carrington, Karen Chavez and Polly McDaniel, our current editor. In 1993, Dr. J. Dan Pittillo asked me to contribute a quarterly "Botanical Excursions" column—also illustrated by Elizabeth—to *Chinquapin: The Newsletter of the Southern Appalachian Botanical Society*. Through the years, Dan, who still edits the publication despite his recent retirement from Western Carolina University, has been an excellent editor, as well as a good friend and supporter. In 2000, I started contributing a weekly "Back Then" regional history column to *Smoky Mountain News*, a newsmagazine published in Waynesville and distributed in the North Carolina counties west of Asheville. Editor Scott McLeod and his staff are to be commended for their efforts in producing this unique and valuable regional publication. All of the essays in this volume have been entirely rewritten.

Elizabeth and I got to know and trust the staff at The History Press when, in 2005, they published my *Mountain Passages: Natural and Cultural History of Western North Carolina and the Great Smoky Mountains*, which displayed one of Elizabeth's paintings on the cover. We were quite pleased when managing editor Kirsten Sutton asked us to undertake this new book, which features even more of Elizabeth's work. And we very much appreciate the level of professionalism Kirsten and her staff display. Brittain Phillips, Julie Foster and Deborah Silliman Wolfe have been especially helpful with this project.

We want to thank Eric Miller for his computer skills and Matt Roark for his map-making expertise. And finally, the input of our youngest daughter, Quintin Ellison, an award-winning journalist with the *Asheville Citizen-Times*, has been invaluable.

I.
The Blue Ridge Province: An Overview

To myself, mountains are the beginning and the end of all natural scenery; in them, and in the forms of inferior landscape that lead to them, my affections are wholly bound up; and though I can look with happy admiration at the lowland flowers, and woods, and open skies, the happiness is tranquil and cold, like that of examining detached wildflowers in a conservatory, or reading a pleasant book; and if the scenery be resolutely level, insisting upon the declaration of its own flatness in all the detail of it...it appears to me a prison, and I can not long endure it.

—JOHN RUSKIN, *MODERN PAINTERS*
(1850)

The Appalachians were uplifted between 250 and 300 million years ago—the period when the massive super continent known as Pangea was being formed via continental drift and plate tectonics. As part of that process, the eastern edge of outlying portions of the North American plate collided head-on with the northwestern edge of the African plate.

Today, the Appalachians extend more than two thousand miles from the Gaspe Peninsula in Canada to north Georgia and north Alabama. How high were these mountains when they were a young and rugged mountain range? Based on discussions with various geologists, my ballpark figure had been 22,000 feet. But one of the foremost Appalachian geologists, Robert D. Hatcher Jr., of the University of Tennessee, a co-author of "Introduction to the Environment and Vegetation of the Southern Blue Ridge Province" (1998), concluded that "around 280–260 [million years ago] the collision of Africa with North America was complete and so was the Appalachian mountain-building process, culminating in a chain *as lofty as any modern mountain chain* [emphasis added]." This would indicate that the original elevation of the young Appalachians approached 30,000 feet—the approximate elevation of peaks in the modern Himalayas. On the other hand, one of the foremost researchers in regard to the topography and natural areas of the Blue Ridge Province, J. Dan Pittillo, now retired from Western Carolina University, recently advised me that, "What it boils down to is the fact that there's no hard evidence in regard to the original elevation of these mountains. No one knows. It may be that both erosion and uplift have been more or less the same so that the original mountain chain was about what it is today in regard to elevation."

For many years, I envisioned the aging of the Appalachians and their Blue Ridge component as an ongoing process in which they would pass through the current phase by gradually eroding into foothills, such as the adjacent Piedmont Province, and then level terrain, such as the Coastal Plain Province. But David Prowell of the U.S. Geological Survey in Atlanta and other geologists are presently considering the possibility that the Appalachians actually started "getting taller" about one hundred million years ago. In an interview with journalist Carlos Santos, Prowell and other geologists discussed this theory.

David Prowell...tells the Richmond Times-Dispatch that the Blue Ridge Mountains are barely rising—a little over 100 feet every million years—but it's enough to offset natural erosion.

"They should have eroded away 100 million years ago...but somehow they are renewing themselves," said Prowell, whose claims have slowly gained support in the scientific community.

"I think it's a new and unique theory," said Scott Southworth, a geologist with the U.S. Geological Survey in Reston [Virginia]. "Mountains don't persist very long... But you look out now and see some pretty high ground from the Smoky Mountains to the Shenandoah. People still refer to the Appalachians as very old mountains, but it's just not true, at least in geological terms."

"Erosion can reduce a mountain chain by 90 percent of its height in 20 million years," Prowell said.

He said that, about 250 million years ago, the African continent pulled away from North America, leaving "gashes" in the earth that filled with tens of thousands of feet of sediment from the eroding mountains. Then our familiar Appalachian Mountains and the Blue Ridge began forming about 140 million years ago, when a westward push of the continental plate started at the mid-Atlantic ridge. That compression is still forcing the mountains to rise, though at such a slight rate that it's not easy to discern.

John Dennison, a geologist at the University of North Carolina, who agrees with Prowell's theory, said the movement of the continental plate is "as fast as a fingernail grows."

Prowell's theory, of course, would mean the Appalachians are relatively young.

"The mountains that now exist aren't the ones that were there in the Paleozoic," he said. "These are new mountains."

Even without the possible intervention of Prowell's westward-crawling continental plate, geologists have contended for years that as mountains erode downward they also, paradoxically, rise upward. Rock is less dense than material lower in the mantle. When mighty mountain ranges are uplifted, the underlying layers of the earth are depressed. As described by Mark W. Carter and the other compilers of *A Geologic Adventure Along the Blue Ridge Parkway in North Carolina* (1999), a "root" develops that helps "buoy up" the less dense mountains. As the mountains erode, pressure is decreased so that simultaneous uplift also occurs. The name for the process is "isostatic rebound."

It's probable that factors other than erosion, isostatic rebound and tectonic plate movement are involved in the ongoing creation of the Blue Ridge Province and adjacent mountainous regions. Out of this sort of complexity, these wondrous mountains are created anew each day. I wholeheartedly agree with Merrill Gilfillan—one of the most rigorous describers of modern American landscapes and a lifelong student of Appalachian topography and ways—in his recent assessment in *Burnt House to Paw Paw: Appalachian Notes* (1997) that, when we venture into the Appalachians, "we have officially entered what geologists call 'the most elegant mountain chain in the world.'"

I consider the Southern Appalachians to be those mountains located south of that point in northeastern Pennsylvania to which glaciers extended eighteen thousand years ago at the height of the last Ice Age. The region is made up of four distinct geographic provinces: Piedmont Province, Ridge and Valley Province, Appalachian Plateau Province and Blue Ridge Province.

The Piedmont Province lies between the Coastal Plain and the Blue Ridge. This belt extends from New Jersey to Georgia, and is about 50 miles wide in its northern portion and from 100 to 150 miles wide in its southern. It is the eroded eastern rim of the ancient Southern Appalachians. Piedmont peaks—sometimes called monadnocks or inselbergs—such as Smith Mountain in Virginia, Pilot Mountain in North Carolina, Parris Mountain in South Carolina and Stone Mountain in Georgia are the remnants of what was once much higher terrain.

The Ridge and Valley Province lies to the west of the Blue Ridge and east of the Appalachian Plateau. It begins in northeast Alabama and northwest Georgia as a broad fertile valley that extends twelve hundred miles northeastward through the Valley of East Tennessee (where Knoxville is located) through Virginia (via the Shenandoah Valley) and continues through portions of West Virginia, Maryland and Pennsylvania before terminating as the Hudson-Champlain Valley in New York. In its northern portions, parallel ridges separated by narrow valleys gave the province its name. In *Field Guide to the Land Forms of the United States* (1972), John A. Shimer provided this description: "From the air the landscape is distinctive and striking. The ridges...extend to the horizon and appear like ordered wave crests, separated by relatively broad, flat troughs." In Pennsylvania and New York, the province extends beyond the Southern Appalachians into the glaciated Northern Appalachians.

The Appalachian Plateau Province extends from northern Alabama into New York state, including portions of Tennessee, Kentucky, Ohio and Pennsylvania. In eastern Ohio, Pennsylvania and New York this province also extends beyond the Southern Appalachians into previously glaciated terrain. The sub-division of the province that extends southward from the Cumberland Gap—where Kentucky, Virginia and Tennessee corner—to a point just south of Birmingham, Alabama, is known as the Cumberland Plateau. Because it was originally a part of the ancient North America plate that predated the Appalachian uplift, some geologists don't consider the Appalachian Plateau Province to be a part of the Southern Appalachians. But the region was so deformed by the cataclysmic events 250 to 300 million years ago, I see no reason to exclude it from the Southern Appalachians.

In regard to mountainous terrain and flora, the Blue Ridge Province is by far the most significant region in eastern North America. It extends about 575 miles from southwest of Harrisburg, Pennsylvania, to the hills of north Georgia. The eastern front of the Blue Ridge is clearly defined from Virginia into South Carolina as a steep escarpment that descends into the adjacent Piedmont. This front reaches its greatest height of 2,500 feet near Blowing Rock, North Carolina. When viewed from a distance, it appears as a continuous blue wall of mountains—the aspect that gave the entire province its name.

Where the Roanoke River passes through a water gap at Roanoke, Virginia, geographers have divided the Blue Ridge into two almost equal sections. North of the water gap, the Northern Blue Ridge Province is a ridge 5 to 15 miles in width and about three thousand feet in elevation. This extends almost 275 miles through central Maryland to a point southwest of Harrisburg, Pennsylvania, where it expires in a series of low ridges.

South of the water gap, the Southern Blue Ridge Province extends southwestward for three hundred miles—encompassing portions of Tennessee, North Carolina and South Carolina—before reaching its terminus at Mount Oglethorpe, about thirty-five miles north of Atlanta. The Southern Blue Ridge is bounded on the east by the range called the Blue Ridge Mountains. On its western front, the province consists of the Iron, Great Smoky, Unocoi and other massive ranges known as the Unakas. Connecting the Blue Ridge Mountain eastern front and the Unakas western front are numerous transverse ranges such as the Blacks, Great Craggies, Newfounds, Great Balsams, Cowees and Nantahalas.

An important factor in the topography of the Southern Blue Ridge is the Eastern Continental Divide. It is the almost imaginary pencil-thin boundary that establishes the divide between waters that flow eastward via various river systems into the Atlantic and those that flow westward via the Tennessee, Ohio and Mississippi River systems to the Gulf of Mexico. Just south of the Roanoke water gap, the divide enters the province at the tiny village of Copper Hill, Virginia. It then winds southward along the Blue Ridge front over the crests of familiar landmarks like Bluff and Grandfather Mountains. In the area of Sassafras Mountain, the divide becomes the boundary between North Carolina and South Carolina. From there, it veers back into North Carolina and traverses Cold Mountain south of Waynesville and numerous peaks in the Highlands, North Carolina, area such as Whiteside, Satulah and Little and Big Scaly Mountains. It then crosses back into Georgia at Rabun Bald and Black Rock State Park, just south of Dillard, Georgia, before entering North Carolina yet again. After circling the Standing Indian basin in the headwaters of the Nantahala River, it passes back into Georgia and follows the Appalachian Trail to Young Lick Knob, at a point about eighteen miles southwest of Clayton, Georgia.

At 3,800 feet in elevation, Young Lick Knob is one of the more inconspicuous peaks along the section of the Appalachian Trail between Dicks Gap (U.S. 76) and Unicoi Gap (GA 75). But geographically it is one of the most significant points in the eastern United States. Here the Eastern Continental Divide reaches its southernmost terminus at a point geographers recognize as a "terminal divide." On the northeastern flank of Young Lick Knob, waters flow into the Atlantic from the Chattooga and Savannah Rivers. On its southeastern flank, waters run directly into the Gulf of Mexico from the Chattahoochee and Apalachicola Rivers. On its western flank, waters follow a long circuitous route to the Gulf via the Hiwassee, Tennessee, Ohio and Mississippi River systems.

The Appalachian system as a whole reaches its greatest elevation, largest mass and most rugged topography in the Southern Blue Ridge, where, according to Marcus B. Simpson Jr., in *Birds of the Blue Ridge Mountains* (1992), "there are 250 mountains over 5,000 feet and 49 that rise above 6,000 feet in elevation." All of those exceeding 6,000 feet are located in either western North Carolina or eastern Tennessee, mostly in North Carolina. Situated northeast of Asheville, North Carolina, Mount Mitchell, at 6,684 feet, is the highest mountain in eastern North America. The terrain of the province becomes even more impressive when you consider that from the North Carolina–Virginia state line northward in the Appalachians to the Gaspe Peninsula in Canada only Mount Washington in New Hampshire exceeds 6,000 feet.

This topography profoundly influences the region's average temperatures—and thereby its plant and animal life, which exhibit strong northern affinities. For each 1,000 feet gained in elevation the mean temperature decreases about four degrees Fahrenheit, equivalent to a change of from 200 to 250 miles in latitude. This means that if you travel from the lowest elevations in the Southern Blue Ridge at about 1,500 feet to the higher elevations above 6,000 feet, it's the equivalent of traveling more than 1,200 miles northward in regard to the habitats you will encounter.

The province is situated where prevailing winds direct warm, water-saturated air masses from the Gulf of Mexico. These air masses are cooled while rising to pass over the Southern Blue Ridge Province, causing condensation to occur. The heaviest amounts of rainfall in the entire Appalachian system have been recorded along the borders of Georgia, North Carolina and South Carolina and in the nearby Great Smoky Mountains. An annual rainfall of 90 inches is not uncommon. As much as 120 to 145 inches of annual rainfall has been recorded in areas within this region, though not every year or always in the same place. Some now refer to the area—which includes Highlands, Cashiers and Brevard, North Carolina—as a "temperate" or "Appalachian" rainforest.

The elevations of the Southern Blue Ridge above four thousand feet can be thought of as a peninsula of northern terrain extending into the southeastern United States, where typical flora and fauna of northeastern and southeastern North America intermingle. Plants and animals that find their southernmost range extensions in the province include Blue Ridge St. John's wort; Canada mayflower; blue-bead lily; pinkshell azalea; witch-hobble; rosebay and purple rhododendron; mountain wood fern; narrow beech fern; lance-leaved and blunt-lobed grape ferns; mountain ash; Table Mountain pine; mountain and striped maples; fire cherry; Fraser magnolia; red spruce; northern flying squirrel; least weasel; woodland jumping mouse; rock vole; New England cottontail; hairy-tailed mole; Smoky shrew; bog turtle; brook trout; muskellunge; saw-whet owl; ruffed grouse; common raven; and Weller's, southern redback, Jordan's, Junauska, shovelnose, longtail, Mountain dusky, imitator, Cherokee and green salamanders. More than a few of these are found only in the province and no place else in the world. Some are only encountered in a few counties.

Birds that winter throughout the southeastern United States but find their southernmost breeding grounds in the Southern Blue Ridge include brown creeper, black-capped chickadee, red-breasted nuthatch, winter wren, golden-crown kinglet, slate-colored junco and others. And long-distance migratory birds such as blue-headed vireo; veery; rose-breasted grosbeak; least flycatcher; and black-throated blue, Canada, chestnut-sided, Blackburnian and golden-winged warblers locate their southernmost breeding grounds in North America in the province. By finding suitable "northern" habitats above four thousand feet elevation this far south in North America, these species eliminate flying hundreds of miles farther north each year, saving both time and energy for breeding efforts.

Through a combination of the processes described above, the Southern Blue Ridge has evolved into the mature upland landscape we can explore today. In doing so, it has become especially diverse in two regards: plant life and natural areas. In the paper he co-authored with geologist Robert D. Hatcher Jr., botanist J. Dan Pittillo summarized the evolution of this plant life and some of its relationships with distinctive natural areas:

The history of the vegetation of the southern Appalachians is as varied as that of the geological record…The North American subcontinent was in a tropical position some 245 to 120 [million years ago] *and evolution and subsequent distribution of ferns, seed ferns, cycads, and gymnosperms* [i.e., plants in which the seeds are not enclosed in an ovary, as is the case with angiosperms, the flowering plants] *probably took place. Of these, only gymnosperms remain dominant in portions of the region today. Angiosperms arose about 120* [million years ago]…*These earlier forests occupied substantially warmer, moister climates than have existed since…the ice ages began* [about two million years ago]. *Many of these* [plants]…*are now isolated in southeastern Asia and southeastern North America, suggesting the great antiquity of the floras of these regions.*

The climate during the glacial periods of the past [two million years] *has varied greatly with average temperatures shifting as much as 18 degrees C between the glacial and interglacial extremes. Such…periods have occurred at about 100 thousand year intervals…*[It has been suggested] *that deciduous forests shifted much farther south* [and] *generalized maps for the past* [forty thousand years] *have shown the presence of spruce* (Picea rubens) *and northern jack pine* (Pinus banksiana) *forests was widespread in the southern Appalachians.* [About eighteen thousand years ago] *the higher peaks may have supported tundra… Following the most recent glacial advance, deciduous forests expanded northward and presumably upward in the Blue Ridge, and the region was dominated by a diverse deciduous mixture around* [ten thousand years ago]. *This warming period continued and the climate became much drier* [between five to six thousand years ago], *perhaps forcing the spruce even higher on the mountain peaks until the cooling period allowed them to drop to their present levels. The contemporary vegetation of the southern Blue Ridge is complex and diverse.*

Pittillo, who has traveled in China to study the relationship between geological changes and the evolution of plant life, noted in passing the many plants "now isolated in southeastern Asia and southeastern North America." The phenomenon is sometimes referred to as "The Asian Connection." In *Hollows, Peepers, and Highlanders: An Appalachian Ecology* (1994), George Constantz devoted an entire chapter to this topic.

"Here's a claim that my surprise you," Constantz wrote. "The forests of eastern Asia and southern Appalachia are so similar that if you were swept from one to the other you would be hard pressed to tell them apart."

He noted that "at the genus and species levels" this similarity "involves more than 50 genera of Appalachian plants—plants that are restricted to eastern North America and eastern Asia and, except in fossil form, are absent in between." The ginseng trade between China and the United States was established during the nineteenth century because of this connection. Plants listed by Constantz with the same or closely related species in both Asia and the Appalachians include tulip poplar, sassafras, yellowwood, silverbell, witch hazel, stewartia, Hercules-club, sumac, persimmon, mayapple, Jack-in-the-pulpit, skunk cabbage and some ferns, lichens and mosses. Others are sweet gum, umbrella leaf, shortia or oconee bells and various species of magnolia and hickory. Constantz also observed that "more than two-thirds of the total orchid genera of temperate North America are related to orchid species in eastern Asia."

Why do we have an Asian connection? Here's the short answer: when the giant super continent of Pangea was formed more than 250 million years ago, numerous plant communities were contiguous across a circumpolar landmass that included Asia, Europe and North America. When Pangea split up some millions of years later, the vestiges of this plant community died out in Europe, eastern Asia and western North America, leaving the Asian and Appalachian communities widely separated. In turn, these remnant communities survived the more recent Ice Age because the Asian mountains and the Southern Appalachians escaped extensive glaciation since both have north-south conformities that resisted the oncoming ice sheets.

According to B. Eugene Wofford's *Guide to the Vascular Plants of the Blue Ridge* (1989), the province presently features upward of 1,500 vascular plants: trees, shrubs, vines, herbs, sedges, grasses, ferns, horsetails, quillworts and club mosses. Many are considered to be showy plants when in flower. There are 130 species of trees in the province, whereas in all of Europe there are only 75 or so species. The primitive non-vascular plants include countless moss and lichen species. And the province is one of the epicenters in the temperate world for mushrooms.

Before the introduction of a non-native fungus around 1910 that decimated the American chestnut trees throughout the Blue Ridge Province, the prototypical forest was "chestnut-heath"; that is, chestnut was the dominant canopy tree, with an understory mainly made up of shrubs such as rosebay rhododendron, mountain laurel and other members of the Heath Family. Before the arrival of the fungus, 30 percent or more of the deciduous forests in the province were made up of chestnut. Almost all of the trees seen in the province now are root sprouts that persist despite the fact that their main trunks have died back to ground level. Within a few years, almost all of these sprouts succumb to the fungus before they can flower and fruit. Today, the prototypical forest of the province is "oak-heath."

The forest types of the present-day Southern Blue Ridge include the spruce-fir or Canadian zone in the highest elevations. It shares characteristics with evergreen forests in eastern Canada and features the most boreal-like climate in the southeastern United States. The conifers that predominate are red spruce and Fraser fir. The latter is being infested and killed by the balsam wooly adelgid, an introduced aphid pest.

Between four and six thousand feet, the northern hardwood zone shares characteristics with the "north woods" of New England. But note that Michael P. Schafale and Alan S. Weakley in their *Classification of the Natural Communities of North Carolina* (1990) made the point that there are clear differences between the two zones:

The name "northern hardwood forest," traditionally given to these communities, implies a similarity to hardwood forests of the northern Appalachians. Many tree, herb, and shrub species are shared; however, our Northern Hardwood Forest has evolved under different climatic regimes, with a different [geographic] history, and has many plant and animal species endemic to the southern Appalachians. It is clearly not the same natural community type as the forests of the northern United States.

Yellow birch and American beech are indicator species for this southern version of the northern hardwood forest, which also features hobblebush, yellow buckeye and mountain maple.

In *Great Smoky Mountains National Park: A Natural History Guide* (1993), Rose Houk described the forest that sometimes appears below the northern hardwood forest in this manner:

> In a place outstanding for diversity of forest types, one type, unique to the southern Appalachians, stands out as the richest of the richest. It is the cove hardwood forest, the forest primeval, one of the most diverse plant communities in the world. The word cove, when used with hardwood forest, refers generally to a sheltered valley, sometimes flat and sometimes steep, below 4,500 feet elevation. Cove soils are rich and deep.

These forests contain an unusually diverse variety of huge trees and lush herbaceous flowering plants. In an anonymous trail guide published by the Great Smoky Mountains National Park, the structure of a cove hardwood forest is described:

> Note how open the lower parts of the forest are and how widely spaced the big trees. The trees that gained a place in the canopy have eliminated their competitors by intercepting sunlight and taking much of the soil moisture and nutrients with their widespread root systems. They allow very few shrubs or tall trees to grow. This is how much of the eastern virgin forest looked—not at all the dense, tangled growth you might have imagined.

The largest and most famous of the cove hardwood forests is Joyce Kilmer Wilderness Area near Robbinsville, North Carolina, just south of the Great Smoky Mountains National Park. Located on U.S. Forest Service lands, the 3,840-acre tract is an amazing site. In *A Directory of North Carolina's Natural Areas* (1987), Charles E. Roe provided this description:

> Massive Canadian hemlocks dominate the forest along the stream flats…but farther upstream give way to mixed hardwoods…Hemlocks measure up to 70 inches in diameter, tulip poplars 76 inches, and oaks 72 inches. Rhododendrons prevail in the forest understory on the flats and ravine bottoms as well as on the ridge top heath balds or "slicks." Green carpets of mosses and liverworts cover boulders, old logs, banks and tree bases in the damp, shaded environments… This classic primeval forest is an exceptional research and recreational source.

Below three thousand or so feet, various pine, oak and hickory species predominate. This type of "pine-oak-hickory" habitat—often made up of Virginia pine, pitch pine or Table Mountain pine, red oak or chestnut oak and pignut hickory—can also appear in higher elevations along exposed slopes and ridges that are relatively dry.

Along streams in the lowest elevations and on moist mountainsides up to four thousand feet, eastern hemlocks form forests called "hemlock ravines." Rosebay rhododendron and other shrubs sometimes form a dense understory. The eastern hemlock along with the endemic Carolina hemlock are both being infested and killed by the hemlock wooly adelgid, another introduced aphid pest.

In addition to these varied forest types, the Southern Blue Ridge comprises a multitude of distinctive natural areas unsurpassed in North America. These include bare granitic domes; wind forests (forests on granitic domes or ridges distinguished by an oak canopy stunted by prevailing high-elevation winds); heath balds (treeless areas dominated by rhododendrons, mountain laurel and other shrubs in the Heath Family that form dense and extensive tangles know locally as "laurel hells"); grassy balds (mysterious treeless areas dominated by grasses, especially mountain oat grass); high-elevation periglacial boulderfields or block streams created at the end of the last Ice Age due to intermittent freezing and thawing; swamp, marsh, bog and fen wetlands; Carolina hemlock bluffs; escarpment gorges; dry vertical cliff systems; spray cliffs; seepage slopes; high-elevation beech gaps; alluvial forests; and floodplain pools.

Living in the heart of the Southern Blue Ridge, as we have for thirty-three years, Elizabeth and I have been fortunate to have ongoing opportunities to explore this wonderland of forest types and natural areas. It is truly a world without end.

(Additional sources for this section are Wallace W. Atwood, *The Physiographic Provinces of North America*; Maurice Brooks, *The Appalachians*; Fred Brown and Nell Jones, *Highroad Guide to the Georgia Mountains*; Fred Byer, *North Carolina: The Years Before Man: A Geologic History*; John A. Conners, *Shenandoah National Park: An Interpretive Guide*; Nevin M. Fenneman, *Physiography of* [the] *Eastern United States*; J. Wright Horton Jr. and Victor A. Zullo, eds., *The Geology of the Carolinas*; Charles B. Hunt, *Natural Regions of the United States and Canada*; Steve Kemp, ed., *Trees & Forests—Great Smoky Mountains National Park*; John C. Kircher, *A Field Guide to the Eastern Forests—North America*; Lynda McDaniel, *Highroad Guide to the North Carolina Mountains*; Harry L. Moore, *A Roadside Guide to the Geology of the Great Smoky Mountains National Park* and *A Geologic Trip Across Tennessee by Interstate 40*; Robert J. Redington, *Survey of the Appalachians*; Michael P. Schafale and Alan S. Weakley, *Classification of the Natural Communities of North Carolina—Third Approximation*; John A. Shimer, *Field Guide to Landforms in the United States*; Vernon and Cathy Summerlin, *Longstreet Highroad Guide to the Tennessee Mountains*; Scott Weidensaul, *Mountains of the Heart: A Natural History of the Appalachians*; Charles H. Wharton, *The Natural Environments of Georgia*; R.H. Whittaker, "Vegetation of the Great Smoky Mountains"; Deane and Garvey Winegar, *Highroad Guide to the Virginia Mountains*; and two anonymous publications—*Cove Hardwood Self-guiding Nature Trail* and *Joyce Kilmer-Slickrock Wilderness and Citico Creek Wilderness in the Nantahala and Cherokee National Forests*.)

II.
Flora

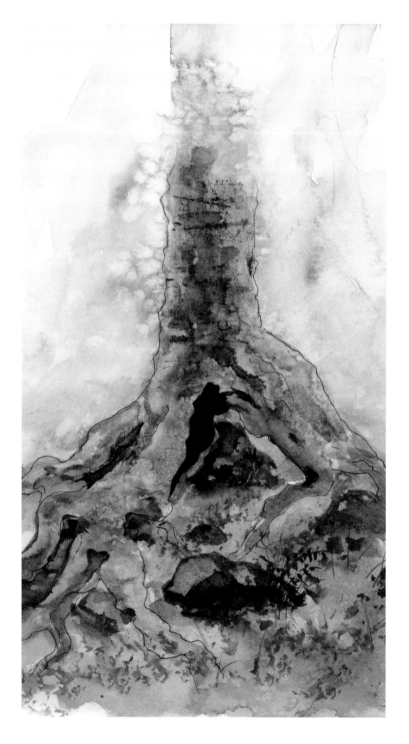

1

THE YELLOW BIRCH AND BOULDER SYNDROME

Do you have favorite trees? I do. Where Elizabeth and I live on the North Carolina side of the Great Smoky Mountains National Park, there are perhaps 120 species. I wouldn't want to do without any of them. In no particular order, however, here are my current top ten: umbrella-leaf magnolia; basswood; Table Mountain pine; mountain ash; butternut walnut; rosebay rhododendron (the only one of the three evergreen rhododendron species native to the Blue Ridge that attains arboreal proportions); chestnut oak; sourwood; black gum; and yellow birch. This time next year, if asked to do so, I would probably come up with a somewhat different list, but yellow birch (*Betula alleghaniensis*) will likely be in my top ten every year for the rest of my life.

On north-facing slopes and in cool ravines or watersheds, yellow birch will sometimes appear in the lower elevations. But it is most common above 3,500 feet, where it becomes my primary indicator species for northern hardwood forests.

Yellow birch can sometimes be tricky to identify. Trees less than two feet in circumference are easy. These display bark that is shiny—yellow or silvery—in color. The bark peels in distinctive papery, horizontal curls that lend the tree a shaggy appearance. Older and larger trees, however, change appearance. The bark loses the telltale horizontal patterning associated with birch species, becoming rough with plate-like scales. If it's winter or the leaves are too high to examine, you can ponder awhile before making an accurate identification. The "yellow" designation in the common name was perhaps derived as much from the tree's rich golden fall foliage as from its bark color. Older trees will sometimes stand until they are little more than sheaths of bark filled with dry punk wood; accordingly, native Americans collected this material and used it as fire tender.

Yellow birch is perhaps the most important lumber species in its genus. Today, its close-grained wood (dark brown to reddish-brown) is used for interior finishes, veneers, tool handles, snowshoe frames and sledges. Formerly it was used for the underwater parts of vessels, ox yokes, bunkhouse logs and hubs that would hold the spokes on wagon wheels more tenaciously than any other wood.

In *The Trees in My Forest* (1997), biologist Bernd Heinrich observed that in New England ruby-throated hummingbirds feed at the "sap wells" yellow-bellied sapsuckers drill in yellow and other birch species. Unable to locate that far north many of the reddish flowers they normally feed upon farther south, hummingbirds not only feed upon birch sap but also on the insects attracted to the wells.

I'm fascinated by yellow birch because of the peculiar tactics it has devised for colonizing various sites. Numerous observers have noted the propensity of yellow birch to germinate upon stumps or fallen logs called "nurse logs" or "mother logs." In *Great Smoky Mountains National Park: A Natural History Guide* (1993), Rose Houk provided a description of the process involved: "Birches often appear to stand on stilts. The prop roots begin to grow when a birch seed falls onto a rotting, moss-covered log. The seed germinates, and as the seedling grows the roots are anchored to the 'nurse log.' Eventually the nurse log decays and disappears, leaving the birch supported on roots that reach out like the arms of an octopus."

Sometimes these stilts will merge, and in that way extend the trunk down to ground level. They can, however, remain as stilts for years. Houk continued with insight regarding this germination-growth strategy: "This interesting habit is almost epiphytic. Epiphytes are the most common in trees in the tropics, where they can survive because of the high humidity and special adaptations that allow them to remove and store water and nutrients from the air. The incredible moisture of the high elevations in the Smokies lets these young birches survive up off the ground. Elsewhere such a habit would lead to excessive water loss, and the tree could not live."

Yellow birch seeds also have the ability to germinate in moss mats that cover large boulders. The ancient high-elevation periglacial boulderfields (sometimes called block streams) found in the Blue Ridge, especially in the higher mountains of western North Carolina and eastern Tennessee, are sometimes entirely colonized by yellow birch. The "guest" literally seals itself to its "host" as its descending stilt roots wrap tightly around the rock and become firmly rooted in the ground below.

One of the most striking instances of this relationship—which I think of as "The Yellow Birch and Boulder Syndrome"—is located in Horse Cove several miles east of Highlands, North Carolina. Near a four-hundred-year-old tulip poplar locally known as the Big Poplar or Bob Padgett Poplar is a very large and old yellow birch that displays scaly bark plates. It's perched high upon a huge boulder, leaning at a seemingly precarious angle toward that spot in the ancient canopy where it originally found light. Some of the stilt roots appear to have actually penetrated the host rock. I am fairly confident that when the tree falls it won't topple off its rocky perch. I'm betting that its tight embrace will upturn the boulder.

In the nooks and crannies of the yellow birch root system that crisscross the boulder, seeds of other species—including rosebay rhododendron, eastern hemlock and tulip poplar—have found adequate soil deposits, germinated and flourished. Rock host and arboreal guests reside there in a harmonious intertwined relationship initiated 250 or more years ago.

2.

TABLE MOUNTAIN PINE:

ARBOREAL EMBLEM

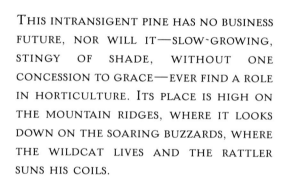

THIS INTRANSIGENT PINE HAS NO BUSINESS
FUTURE, NOR WILL IT—SLOW-GROWING,
STINGY OF SHADE, WITHOUT ONE
CONCESSION TO GRACE—EVER FIND A ROLE
IN HORTICULTURE. ITS PLACE IS HIGH ON
THE MOUNTAIN RIDGES, WHERE IT LOOKS
DOWN ON THE SOARING BUZZARDS, WHERE
THE WILDCAT LIVES AND THE RATTLER
SUNS HIS COILS.

—DOUGLAS CULROSS PEATTIE, *A NATURAL
HISTORY OF TREES OF EASTERN AND CENTRAL
NORTH AMERICA* (1950)

Have you ever been walking one of the wind-swept, sun-bitten, high-elevation rock outcrops in the Blue Ridge when you suddenly encountered a grove of strange, almost stunted-looking pines with outlandish cones? As described by Douglas Culross Peattie, they bear "huge cones that encircle the limbs in dense clusters, each knob of the cone armed with a horrendous hooked prickle, as if to guard the harsh fruit."

If so, you will have happened upon Table Mountain pine (*Pinus pungens*), one of the six pine species native to the Blue Ridge. The others are white pine, pitch pine, short-leaf pine, Virginia or scrub pine and loblolly pine. Of these, Table Mountain pine is the one that is essentially restricted to the Southern Appalachians, most particularly to the Blue Ridge.

According to Claud A. Brown and L. Katherine Kirkman's *Trees of Georgia and Adjacent States* (1990), the essential range of this species extends from central Pennsylvania southwest to eastern West Virginia, on down through southwestern Virginia into the mountainous terrains of western North Carolina and eastern Tennessee and then, just barely, into the fringes of northwestern South Carolina and northeastern Georgia. Toward the southern end of its range, the tree reaches its highest elevation at 5,780 feet in the Great Smoky Mountains National Park, where a stunted individual grows upon Andrews Bald.

Some sources state that the species is known as Table Mountain pine because it thrives on gravelly tablelands, ridges and slopes. Others assert that the name is derived from the fact that the species was first collected about 1794 near Table Rock Mountain in Burke County, North Carolina. It is also known as bur or prickly pine (because of the cones), mountain pine, hickory pine (because of limbs that are, as Peattie described them, "elastic but unbreakable by human muscle") and squirrel pine (because the seeds are favored by red squirrels, locally known as "boomers").

The tree flourishes where there is site disturbance, light and heat. In closed stands on western and northern exposures, the cones are distinctly serotinous; that is, they require heat from a fire before opening to release seed. On southerly and easterly exposures, however, many cones open soon after maturing. A large number of closed cones remain on the serotinous trees for five to twenty-five years, with the retained seeds remaining viable for ten or more years. This pine has limited human uses as pulpwood and low-grade charcoal. On the other hand, it provides seeds for wildlife on a year-round basis.

It is asserted on various Internet sites that lyricist Ballard Macdonald, whose most famous song perhaps was "Beautiful Ohio", had a Table Mountain pine in mind when, in 1913, he penned the words to "In the Blue Ridge Mountains of Virginia":

In the Blue Ridge Mountains of Virginia
On the trail of the lonesome pine
In the pale moonshine our hearts entwine
Where she carved her name and I carved mine.
Oh, June, like the mountains I'm blue
Like the pine I am lonesome for you
In the Blue Ridge Mountains of Virginia
On the trail of the lonesome pine.

The songwriter called it a "lonesome pine," and that is perhaps an apt description. For the ancient Cherokees, however, Table Mountain pine was a symbol of health and long life. It is a wonderful tree—one that, in my opinion, should be the arboreal emblem of the Blue Ridge.

3.

BLACK GUM:

RABBIT TRAPS AND BEE GUMS

THE WILDERNESS, ROUGH, HARSH, AND
INEXORABLE, HAS CHARMS MORE POTENT
IN THEIR SEDUCTIVE INFLUENCE THAN
ALL THE LURES OF LUXURY AND SLOTH.
AND OFTEN HE ON WHOM IT HAS CAST
ITS MAGIC FINDS NO HEART TO DISSOLVE
THE SPELL.

—FRANCIS PARKMAN, *HISTORY OF THE
CONSPIRACY OF PONTIAC* (1851)

The ancient Cherokees and, subsequently, the white settlers here in the Blue Ridge lived close to the natural world. In some ways, of course, it was a cold, messy and even, at times, cruel existence. But in other ways such a life must have also been very rewarding. You and I have to flip a switch in our minds in order to shift from our modern technological ambiance to make some sort of connection with our natural environments. Every single day, for better or worse, those folks woke up as an integrated part of the glorious world that surrounded them.

They were attentive to all aspects of the land—landscapes, flora and fauna—because these provided the basics for survival and the necessary commodities for creature comforts. Back then, medicines, foods, dyes and building materials couldn't be purchased at Lowe's or Wal-Mart or even local pharmacies, groceries or hardware stores. It's my supposition that because they had to pay closer attention to the everyday world the Cherokees and early settlers felt closer to and more at home in that world than many of us do today. In this regard, let's consider first how the early settlers used hollow black gum trees for multiple purposes, and then, in the following essay, how they made sled runners from sourwood trees.

First, some botanical background is in order. Most people associate black gum or tupelo (also called black tupelo, bowl gum, gum, pepperidge, sour gum, stinkwood, swamp gum, swamp tupelo, tupelo gum, yellow gum, yellow gum tree, wild pear tree and other names) with swamps and moist low-lying areas, not mountainous terrain. Indeed, the initial black gum variety taxonomically described as *Nyssa sylvatica* was a swamp-growing type, with the generic name assigned in honor of Nyssa, the mythological Greek water nymph. The specific epithet means "of the woods." As for the common name black gum, the first part refers to the dark leaves, but no one seems to know for sure what the designation "gum" referred to originally. Tupelo was derived from *ito opilwa*, the Creek Indian name for the tree.

There are, however, two varieties of *N. sylvatica* that botanists now recognize—based on variances in leaf shapes, fruit sizes, seed characteristics and preferred habitats. One can be aptly distinguished as swamp tupelo (*N. sylvatica* var. *biflora*) since it grows in wet woods and swamps. The only region it has been located in the Blue Ridge is in the northwestern corner of South Carolina. When occurring in frequently flooded sites, the bases of the trunks for this variety are usually swollen, as is the instance with cypress trees.

To the other variety (*N. sylvatica* var. *sylvatica*) we can apply the common name black gum. It grows throughout the eastern United States, being common in dry sites throughout the Blue Ridge (often in oak and pine forests) up to five thousand feet elevation or more. Black gum, which can be a hundred feet tall, is usually somewhat larger than swamp tupelo. During the fall color season, its leaves turn an eye-catching lipstick red. The wood possesses an interlocked grain—so that, much like sycamore, it just about can't be split, not even with the use of wedges. Accordingly, the early settlers used the wood for mauls, tool handles, skid poles and rough floors for outbuildings.

Now we get to the interesting part. Perhaps every other mature black gum tree here in the Blue Ridge is to a greater or lesser extent hollow. This is because the species is highly susceptible to heart rot fungi. This infection occurs when aerially disseminated spores from various decay fungi are deposited on or near fire scars or dead branch stubs of susceptible hosts. After these spores germinate, the fungi's vegetative strands (mycelium) grow slowly into the vulnerable wood tissues. The fungi that invade black gum attack only the tree's central column of physiologically inactive (non-living) heartwood. An infected tree retains its outer vascular tissues for support and nutrient transport, but internally it becomes hollow.

For wild critters, hollow black gum trees make wonderful nest and refuge sites. For the Cherokees and early settlers, they represented a utilitarian item that could be used in numerous ways. Sections were fitted with bottoms and made into containers. They also served as pipes or troughs for channeling or diverting water. Pits or wells could be cased at the surface with a hollow black gum log in order to prevent an inflow of surface water.

A small hollowed section of black gum could also be closed at one end, fitted with a triggered sliding door at the other end, baited and used as a rabbit trap. When I was a boy, an uncle of mine showed me how to make these traps, which he called "rabbit gums." I did catch the occasional rabbit, but most of the time, when I turned the trap up on its back end and slid the door open to see what was inside, there was a possum staring up at me. That was OK. My grandmother paid twenty-five cents per possum, which she placed in a cage, "fatted up" for a couple of weeks on vegetables and then baked along with sweet potatoes.

But the most noteworthy use of hollow black gum logs was as "bee gums" that became a haven for honeybees and a source of "sweetenin'." Their construction is described in some detail in *Foxfire 2* (1973), a volume compiled and edited by Elliott Wigginton and his high school students in north Georgia:

> *Hollow sections of the tree would be brought home and the inside rounded out smooth and uniform with a long chisel. "Middleways" of the gum, four holes would be bored— one at each point of the compass—and two sticks run horizontally through the gum at right angles to each other. These sticks acted as supports from which the bees would suspend their brood combs. The bees would automatically save the top half of the gum for their honey and would hang those combs from the plank lid, or "head," that was set over the top of the gum. The head was often held in place by a stick run through two wooden eyes…Then a slanted, easily removable lid was usually set above the head to keep rain from running into the gum. Beekeepers always set the gums on flat platforms. Small rocks could be set under one edge of the gum tilting it slightly so the bees could enter; or "V"-shaped notches were cut into the bottom on one side to serve the same purpose. The platform extended several inches beyond the entrance to provide a landing area.*

Most hives these days are prefabricated, box-shaped units. But throughout the nineteenth century and into the early twentieth century, black gum hives were prevalent in the Blue Ridge backcountry.

As related on the Internet site titled *Will Walker—Legend of Tuckaleechee Cove*, William Marion ("Big Will") Walker moved with his wife, Nancy Louisa Caylor Walker, into the wilderness of Middle Prong of Little River in east Tennessee the year they were married in 1859. Walker felled and hewed logs and put them up for the house when they first moved into the valley—a home that sheltered them for all sixty years of their marriage. It's recorded that "Will had 75 stands of bees in only one location, at a place he called the 'Blowdown,' where the wind had felled a grove of poplar trees several miles upstream from their home. Most of the bees at this location and others were in sections of hollow black gum logs—bee gums. Will sold big quantities of honey."

4.

SOURWOOD:

NATURAL BENDS
AND SLED RUNNERS

Sourwood, one of my favorite trees, comes into full bloom throughout the Blue Ridge in mid-summer. You can easily identify this graceful member of our flora by its long elliptical leaves and white drooping flowering tassels that remind me of lily-of-the-valley. The soft green sourwood leaves, which display distinctively patterned veins, are particularly attractive. The wood is hard, featuring red-tinged brown heartwood and very thick layers of paler sapwood. Mature sourwood trees growing in optimum conditions are usually about 50 to 60 feet tall. One that grew (and may still be growing) on U.S. Forest Service property near Robbinsville, North Carolina, stood 118 feet high with a circumference of 77 inches.

Sourwood (*Oxydendron arboreum*) belongs to the Heath Family (*Ericaceae*), which is one of the most interesting and important plant families. It is composed of about 2,500 species that are widely distributed throughout the world. In the Blue Ridge there are about fifty species. These vary greatly in regard to both size and appearance: rhododendron, laurel, trailing arbutus, wintergreen, pipsissewa, highland doghobble, fetterbush, shinleaf, blueberry, maleberry, minniebush, sand myrtle, pinesap, Indian pipe and more.

Rosebay rhododendron sometimes attains arboreal proportions, but sourwood is the only member of the Heath Family in our area that is always classified as a tree. How curious to realize that it is closely related to Indian pipe, which dwells in the leaf-litter and muck low down on the forest floor. Urn-shaped flowers made up of four to five petals are a characteristic all species of the family display.

The common name sourwood is derived from the acrid taste of its leaves. It is also known as arrowwood, elk tree, sour gum, lily-of-the-valley tree and sorrel gum. Paul Hamel and Mary Chiltoskey reported in *Cherokee Plants: Their Uses—A 400 Year History* (1975) that sourwood was used by the Cherokees medicinally as a tonic, tea or "bark ooze" for indigestion, asthma, lung diseases, diarrhea, itch, mouth ulcers and "nerves." The early white settlers learned these uses from the Cherokees, and they also employed extracts for kidney and bladder ailments. In general, the Cherokees and settlers used the leaves in summer and the bark (green or dry) in winter. Much of the plant's reputation as a medicine—whether deserved or not—can be attributed to the presence of organic acids.

The Cherokees also used sourwood to craft pipe stems, arrow shafts and butter paddles. The white settlers crafted various tool handles from the wood, but, more importantly, they immediately noticed that the trunk of a mature sourwood has a natural bend about mid-way to two-thirds of the way above the ground. Bingo!—they needed runners for their sleds—sourwood is hard and smooth—it was practically a no-brainer. In no time they began felling and sectioning the sourwood trees so as to incorporate this natural curve into the required shape for the runners on their oxen- or mule-drawn sleds.

I've known about this use of sectioned sourwood for sled runners for years. But I have also pondered the cause of this natural bend for almost a like number of years. Every time I went into the field with a botanist or another naturalist, I would quiz them about the sourwood's natural bend. Every time I was met with glazed expressions. One notable botanist suggested that I use a compass to see "if they always bend toward the rising sun."

I did. They don't.

One fine spring day several years ago, I was conducting a natural history workshop with my friend and colleague Murray Evans, now retired from his position as a professor in the biology department at the University of Tennessee in Knoxville. In addition to being an authority on the ferns of North America, Murray is also a noted taxonomist; that is, he was trained to pay special attention to the relationships of plants and categorize them accordingly.

"Murray," I asked as we led the group along a trail near Highlands, North Carolina, "do you see that bend way up there in that sourwood tree? Most mature sourwoods do that—I've been wondering for years why they have that bend. No one seems to know."

"Oh, I think I might," he replied rather matter-of-factly. "You've got to remember that sourwood is a member of a plant family comprised mostly of shrubs. Sourwood *decided* to be a tree, but it has retained some of the characteristic growth patterns of a shrub. See how the limbs tend to arch out and then downward like a shrub? And that natural bend in the trunk is also shrub-like. That's what I think."

"Thanks," I responded. My curiosity was at last satisfied.

One just about can't see sourwood trees in bloom without thinking of the fresh honey that's in the making. Stand under a sourwood in full bloom and you'll hear what has been called the "song of summer" coming from the congregation of bees feeding high above. The honey is extra-light to light amber color and extremely aromatic, with a distinctive rich flavor. In local markets throughout the Blue Ridge, it commands a premium price. Many residents of the region swear that, when it comes to quality and taste, no other honey can match sourwood honey.

5.

SARVIS:
WHAT'S IN A NAME?

The tree known as Allegheny serviceberry, Juneberry, shadbush, shadblow and sugarplum in other parts of the country is referred to throughout the Blue Ridge as *sarvis* or related forms such as *sarviceberry*, *sarvisberry*, *sarvissberry*, *sarviss tree* or *sarviss*. This supposedly colloquial pronunciation of "service" is often attributed to the fact that the tree's early blooms signaled the arrival of the traveling preacher, who would hold the year's first formal commemoration for those who had been unable to survive the winter. But tracking the precise origins of the designation *sarvis* and its related forms is actually more complicated than that.

Serviceberry is a member of the Rose Family (*Rosaceae*), along with chokeberry, hawthorn, apple, plum, pear, mountain ash, rose and others. From as early as mid-March in the lower elevations into June in the higher elevations, the showy white flowers with their ribbon-like petals are frequently so numerous on the tree's bare limbs that the trees seem covered with snow.

There are five serviceberry species in the Blue Ridge. Only two of these are common throughout. Downy serviceberry (*Amelanchier aborea*) is usually found below three thousand feet. Its leaves, generally heart-shaped at the base, are covered underneath with white hairs during the flowering period. The fruits are reddish purple. These are dry and not tasty to humans, although birds seem to like them just fine. Smooth serviceberry

(*A. laevis*) is found from the lowest elevations to six thousand or so feet. Its leaves, which are generally not heart-shaped at the base, are hairless. The fruits that appear from June into August are dark purple, juicy and tasty to humans and birds alike. But beating the birds to them is just about impossible as they are usually situated far above human reach.

The wood of the smooth serviceberry tree, which ranges from twenty to thirty feet in height, is strong, close-grained and very heavy. It's the fifth hardest of all the woods in the United States and takes a beautiful polish. Because of its small size, however, the tree is rarely logged and normally used only for tool handles.

The common names Juneberry and sugarplum are self-evident. Allegheny is a reference to its presence in the mountainous regions of Pennsylvania and adjacent states. In coastal areas, it's known as shadbush because the spring migration of shad from the ocean into upland freshwater streams occurs in early spring when serviceberry is blooming. And in the same region it's sometimes called shadblow because the word "blow" can have the meaning of "in a state of blossoming."

The most frequently heard explanation for the colloquial designation *sarvis* usually goes something like the one provided by John Parris in *Mountain Bred* (1967):

> As cabins were grooved together and the land cleared, the women-folks planted their flower seeds and waited for blooming time. But while they waited they looked to the appearance of wild flowers for their funeral wreaths and wedding decorations. But in a land where winter was long and spring came late the wild flowers were late in coming, too. The women-folks who came first, who came and settled between the flowering seasons, were the ones to notice the spring-heralding flowers of the high-mountain forest trees for which they had no names. They gathered them and carried them to church services and funeral services. And because these trees provided flowers for the services they called them "sarvis," which was to say service. Thus it was that the word

caught on and came to stand for spring's first blooming tree in the mountains.

Along these same lines, retired Western Carolina University botanist Jim Horton provided additional information in *The Summer Times* (1979): "Several explanations are advanced for the common name…The most interesting, though not necessarily the most accurate, holds that the tree blooms during 'service' time; the time when old-timey itinerant preachers were first penetrating the mountains after the spring thaw and performing services: baptizing babies born during the winter, performing marriages (probably legitimizing the babies baptized) and the like."

But there are several other related explanations. In *A Natural History of Trees of Eastern and Central North America* (1950), naturalist Donald Culross Peattie, who lived in the Blue Ridge for a time during the 1940s near Tryon, North Carolina, provided this derivation: "It is from the fruits that the Sarvissberry takes its name, for the word is a transformation of the 'sorbus' given by the Romans to a related kind of fruit. Sarviss is a good Shakespearean English form of the most classic Latin, whereas Serviceberry is meaningless as a name, or at least a genteel corruption of an older and more scholarly form." For good measure, I'll also note that *The Compact Edition of the Oxford English Dictionary* (1971) cites *sarves* as a variant form of *service*, when applied to one of the European pear trees (*Pyrus domestica*).

I suspect there's a bit of truth in all of these versions. A North American tree came to be known as serviceberry along the eastern seaboard because its fruits were similar to the European *sorbus* tree—then, here in the Blue Ridge, several species of this tree just happened to bloom in profusion when their flowers were handy for spring ceremonials such as funeral services and became known as *sarvis*. Curiously enough, that regional colloquialism for service apparently wasn't newly minted here but represented the revival of *sarves*, an older form of the word that had originated in the Old World.

6.

AZALEAS AND RHODODENDRONS

Azaleas and rhododendrons are the signature plants of the Blue Ridge. They attract our attention throughout the year with their beauty as well as by their distinctive pollination and over-wintering strategies. Many participants in my plant identification workshops are puzzled by the distinction between a rhododendron and an azalea. They're not sure whether they are the same or separate entities. That's because rhododendrons and azaleas were at one time classified separately within the Heath Family (*Ericaceae*). The shrubs classified in the *Rhododendron* genus displayed evergreen leaves, a short corolla tube and ten stamens. Those in the *Azalea* genus displayed deciduous leaves, a long corolla tube and five stamens. But as plant hunters began to explore worldwide, especially in Asia during the nineteenth century, they discovered rhododendrons with azalea characteristics and vice versa. It became apparent that taxonomically the generic groups couldn't remain separated, so the azaleas were reclassified as various species in the *Rhododendron* genus. For instance, the scientific name for the shrub known as flame azalea is *Rhododendron calendulaceum*.

In the Blue Ridge there are three evergreen rhododendron species: rosebay rhododendron (*R. maximum*), purple rhododendron (*R. catawbiense*) and Carolina rhododendron (*R. minus*).

Rosebay rhododendron is the most common. It grows alongside low-elevation streams and into the higher elevations in woodland settings. The flowers are white or pinkish-white. The leaves are six to twelve inches long with pointed tips. Rosebay is the only evergreen or deciduous species in the genus that can attain arboreal proportions and is, therefore, listed in many tree identification guides. The others are always categorized as shrubs.

The showiest of the evergreen rhododendrons is the purple rhododendron. The leaves are four to six inches long with rounded tips. It grows as a compact shrub on rocky slopes, ridges and balds above three thousand feet. It is also called Catawba rhododendron. According to legend, the Catawba Indians once challenged all of the other Indian nations to a great battle in the mountains in early summer. After many days of battle, the Catawbas were victorious—but in the fighting they shed so much precious blood that these rhododendrons have bloomed red ever since in mute tribute to their sacrifice.

As I noted in my essay "John Fraser and the Economics of Plant Exploration" in *Mountain Passages* (2005), the economic considerations behind the botanical exploration of the southern mountains have been generally neglected. An almost insatiable desire on the part of Europeans, especially in England, for American plants emerged during the late eighteenth century. Commercial nurseries were founded that vied with one another for the introduction of choice plants. The point men for the nursery owners were designated plant collectors who traveled far and wide in a competitive hunt for new plants. Of the numerous prized plants they discovered in the Blue Ridge, purple rhododendron was surely the foremost. John Fraser, a Scotsman from Inverness-shire, was, from 1786 until 1807, one of the European plant hunters most closely associated with the southern mountains. It was Fraser who—after making extensive collections of purple rhododendron on Roan Mountain—first promoted its horticultural use in England, where numerous hybrid forms were quickly developed. In time, cold-tolerant hybrids of our native purple rhododendron called "ironclads" returned to America as cultivars that could then be marketed far and wide, including such profitable areas as New England and other northern climes.

Carolina rhododendron—also called dwarf or piedmont rhododendron, as well as deer-tongue laurel—is the evergreen rhododendron with which people are least familiar. As a straggling upright shrub, it grows in the higher elevations with its Catawba cousin or in the lower elevations with its rosebay cousin. The flowers are magenta in color. The leaves are short and rough, with conspicuous brown scales on the undersides. Various growth forms used to be classified as separate species (*R. carolinianum* or *R. punctatum*) but today they are lumped together as a single species (*R. minus*). The variant forms are probably the result of non-genetic environmental factors. Naturalist Arthur Stupka noted in *Trees, Shrubs, and Woody Vines of Great Smoky Mountains National Park* (1964) that dwarf specimens which appear at elevations above 4,500 feet in the Smokies normally flower during late June and early July, while at elevations below 2,500 feet larger specimens of up to ten feet in height flower from mid-May to mid-June.

Many visitors to the Blue Ridge arrive in mid-spring hoping to observe rhododendrons and azaleas in full bloom. They return home disappointed. The peak flowering period for this group of plants is usually mid-June.

All of the evergreen rhododendrons display yellow or green spots on their uppermost petal. These function as nectar guides for bumblebees, moths and other insects that pollinate the plants. It's probable that the spots appear iridescent in the eyes of these insects and literally serve as beacon lights. Honeybees, bumblebees and other large insects can force their way into the cupped blossoms so as to access the nectar cached deep in the flower tube.

The largest and most interesting pollinator of rosebay rhododendron is the hawk moth. Sometimes called sphinx moths, these insects look like hummingbirds or bumblebees but are the airborne form of the different hornworm species that, as caterpillars, ravage tomato, tobacco and other crops. They can have wingspans more than five inches that beat up to thirty times a second as they hover at dusk and into the night seeking nectar sources. Equipped with exceptionally long tongues, the sphinx moths easily penetrate the deepest flowering recesses. Glimmering luminously in the woodlands through the long summer nights, rosebay rhododendron flowers provide the perfect nectar opportunity for these moths.

Evergreen rhododendron species have evolved distinctive over-wintering devices. Their shrubby growth forms and flexible limbs usually withstand the heaviest snowfalls, even blizzards. Their thick leaves have waxy coats that cut down on evaporation. To avoid having their leaf cells ruptured by frost, water is channeled to spaces between the cells where expansion does less damage. The sugar content of the cells is increased to lower freezing levels. And the leaves of rosebay rhododendron droop and curl in extreme cold. Some old-timers even claim they can tell how cold it is by how much the leaves droop. Be that as it may, the drooping tactic obviously lessens exposure to wind, while the curling temporarily shields and closes off air-circulation pores (stomata) on the underside of the leaves.

In the Blue Ridge there are eight deciduous rhododendron species: flame azalea, pinkshell azalea, pink azalea, smooth azalea, Cumberland azalea, pink or pinxter-flower azalea, early azalea and clammy azalea. Here is a closer look at the first two of these species.

Flame azalea (*R. calendulaceum*) is one of our most magnificent flowering plants. Produced in profusion on low-growing twiggy shrubs that are often as wide as they are tall, its funnel-shaped blossoms, which range in color from red to yellow to orange and all shades in between, illuminate woodland glades. William Bartram, the pioneer botanist in the Blue Ridge, observed flame azalea in north Georgia in 1775 and described "this most celebrated species of azalea" in his *Travels Through North & South Carolina, Georgia, East & West Florida* (1791) as being "in general of the color of the finest red lead, orange and bright gold, as well as yellow and cream color; these various splendid colors are not only in separate plants but on branches on the same plant; and the clusters of the blossoms cover the shrubs in such incredible profusion on the hillsides that suddenly opening to view from dark shades, we are alarmed with apprehension of the hill being set on fire. This is certainly the most gay and brilliant shrub yet known."

The varied colors that flame azalea blossoms display are sometimes attributed to the possibility that shrubs without the same colored blossoms are growing in different soil types. But variations occur on plants that are often standing side by side in the same type of soil. And, as William Bartram noted, color variations even occur on the same plant. Many biologists now think the explanation is that over a period of time—in different light and weather conditions—plants have a better chance of attracting a more dim set of pollinators for cross-fertilization by displaying a spectrum of flower colors. For instance, the so-called confederate violet is simply a white-gray color morph of the common blue violet—a variation that allows the species to attract pollinators under dim light conditions. The array of colors displayed by morning glory blossoms serves as another example. All of them—no matter the color—belong to the same species. As beautiful to our eyes as the blossoms of flame azalea and other showy flowering plants are, they were not devised for our pleasure but to beguile pollinators. Displaying color morphs is most likely just another of their myriad strategies.

The uncommonly beautiful pinkshell azalea (*R. vaseyi*) is found no place else in the world but the Blue Ridge. Indeed, it's restricted in its native range to high-elevation bogs and the edges of spruce-fir forests in seven counties in western North Carolina. Before their leaves emerge, these graceful shrubs, standing three to fifteen feet tall, display pink flowers that are almost translucent. One of the most impressive displays can usually be viewed in late May along the Blue Ridge Parkway between Balsam Gap and Mount Pisgah. They are especially apparent near Haywood Gap between mileposts 426 and 427.

In *The Summer Times* (1979), botanist Jim Horton noted that pinkshell azalea is "interesting as a transitional form between the rhododendrons and azaleas that are now considered to be members of the same genus…Pinkshell azalea has the deciduous leaves of the Azaleas, the short corolla tube (less than ¼ the length of the lobes) of the Rhododendron and usually produces 7 stamens. It is partly what convinced botanists to combine the two groups."

7.

HIGHLAND DOGHOBBLE:

THE BLACK BEAR'S REFUGE

RHODODENDRONS GROW IN MANY
LOCATIONS...OFTEN IN VERY SHADY PLACES.
THE SAME IS TRUE OF DOGHOBBLE. BOTH
OF THESE SHRUBS HAVE RELATIVELY THICK,
DARK GREEN LEAVES THAT REFLECT LESS
LIGHT THAN LIGHT-COLORED LEAVES SUCH
AS THOSE OF MAPLE AND POPLAR. THESE
THICK LEAVES ABSORB ALMOST ALL THE
LIGHT THAT FALLS UPON THEM, ENABLING
THE PLANTS TO SURVIVE IN WEAKER LIGHT.
—ROSS HUTCHINS, *HIDDEN VALLEY OF THE*
SMOKIES (1971)

Whenever I'm conducting a native plant identification workshop, I try to note several regional plants—one each in the fern, shrub and tree categories—that participants might use effectively in an ornamental setting. For a fern, I usually recommend cinnamon fern (*Osmunda cinnamomea*). For a small tree, sweet pepperbush is my favorite (*Clethra acuminata*). And highland doghobble (*Leucothoe fontanesiana*) is certainly an attractive and manageable shrub that has interesting associations in regard to both its common and scientific names.

Sometimes called drooping leucothoe, switch ivy or fetterbush, highland doghobble is one of the more common shrubs in the southern mountains, especially the Blue Ridge portions of North Carolina, Tennessee, South Carolina and Georgia. Several other closely related species, coastal doghobble (*L. axillaries*) and swamp doghobble (*L. racemosa*), are found mostly in lowland situations. Highland doghobble flourishes in shade in acidic soils alongside low-elevation streams and on mountainsides into the higher elevations. Its long arching branches often cover entire slopes, frequently in association with rosebay rhododendron and mountain laurel.

The alternate leaves of highland doghobble are evergreen and rather sharply toothed. From late April into June, dense clusters of bell-shaped white flowers—which can be quite showy and fragrant—appear toward the tips of the branches. In autumn, the buds that will produce next year's flowers form where the leaves are attached to the main stem. As winter advances, these buds display an eye-catching dark red color.

But it's the arching branches that are doghobble's primary claim to fame. These often root at their tips, creating an extensive tangle that is almost impenetrable. A black bear fleeing hunting dogs will intuitively head for a doghobble tangle situated on a steep slope, which it can easily bound through going upgrade. Pursuing dogs and hunters are quickly left behind, "doghobbled" by the rooted branches and sharp leaves.

Highland doghobble is a member of the Heath Family (*Ericaceae*), which includes rhododendrons, laurels and numerous other plants that are mostly shrubs. Sourwood is the only tree in the family. The story behind the generic designation *Leucothoe* (leu-koth-o-e) is related by Ovid, the Roman author who lived at the time of Christ, in his *Metamorphoses*. Leucothoe's father, Orachamus, was so enraged when he discovered that she had given herself to Apollo that he "cruelly buried her in a living grave, and piled a heavy heap of sand on top." The distraught Apollo could not bring her back to life, so "he sprinkled her body, and the spot where it lay, with perfumed nectar," exclaiming "'You will reach heaven, none the less!'" Sure enough, her perfumed body dissolved away, "soaking the earth with sweet-scented essence" and "a shrub of incense spread its roots down

through the earth, and itself rose into the air, its shoots breaking through the mound."

Elizabeth and I have never purchased doghobble because our creek's banks and adjacent woodlands are covered with the plant. We can, however, easily envision its use as an ornamental border for a walkway or around a patio—or maybe as a backdrop in a partially shaded area for lower-growing herbaceous plants. Horticulture specialist Richard Bir described the shrub's potential role as an ornamental in *Growing and Propagating Showy Native Woody Plants* (1992):

> *The best garden leucothoes are grown for their foliage rather than flowers. Drooping leucothoe will have dark glossy foliage year round in the shade. If planted where it receives some sunlight in winter, foliage will turn bronze to burgundy following the first frost. New growth is often quite red, with the selection "Scarletta" probably having the reddest. A variegated selection, "Girard's Rainbow," is becoming widely available.*

8

GALAX:

ODIFEROUS AND DECORATIVE

THIS IS THEIR NATIVE COUNTRY, AND THE
GALAX IS A WILD FOLIAGE PLANT WHICH
GROWS ON THE BLEAK SIDES AND SUMMITS
OF THE BIG MOUNTAINS...IT HAS A RICH
GREEN COLOR IN THE SUMMER, WHICH
DEEPENS INTO A SPLENDID BRONZE AS THE
WINTER APPROACHES. THESE LEAVES...ARE
USED IN THE HOMES OF THE RICH PEOPLE IN
THE CITIES FOR DECORATION. DURING THE
FALL AND WINTER, THE POOR PEOPLE FIND
EMPLOYMENT AND SMALL COMPENSATION IN
GATHERING THE LEAVES AND SELLING THEM,
AT FROM FIFTEEN TO TWENTY-FIVE CENTS A
THOUSAND. IT IS A HARD WAY TO MAKE A
LIVING, ESPECIALLY WHEN SNOW AND ICE
COVER THE MOUNTAINS, AND WHEN THE
LEAVES ARE MOST VALUABLE. PROBABLY NONE
WHO ENJOY THEIR GORGEOUS FOLIAGE IN A
STATELY MANSION EVER KNOW WHAT LABOR
AND SACRIFICE AND SUFFERING THESE LEAVES
COST THE POOR HIGHLANDERS.

—EDWARD GUERRANT, *THE GALAX GATHERERS:*
THE GOSPEL AMONG THE HIGHLANDERS (1910)

Galax (*Galax urceolata*) is an evergreen groundcover found throughout the Blue Ridge. The plant can thrive in various settings, but the ideal habitat is a cool moist site with partial shade and acidic soil. It occurs in extensive patches that can reward the observer in every season. As Peter White observed in *Wildflowers of the Smokies* (1996), "In early spring, its round, evergreen leaves carpet the dormant forest floor. By summer, a tall pillar of tiny white flowers line many park trails. Then, as winter approaches, the deep green leaves turn bronze and crimson to contrast against the coming snows."

During the early 1900s, many residents of southwestern Virginia and northwestern North Carolina gathered and sold galax leaves that were shipped out by rail for use as ornamentals. An official from the Norfolk and Western Railway Company observed this activity and suggested that one of the communities in the area be named for the plant. In 1906, the Virginia General Assembly officially chartered the town of Galax, Virginia.

Two attributes of galax are of particular interest: the odor it sometimes exudes and the colors its leaves exhibit each fall.

Have you ever been walking a mountain trail and encountered a musky smell that reminded you of skunk, mold or scat? Whenever this happens, I consider six possible sources: skunk, bear scat, wild boar rooting, carrion vine (*Smilax herbacea*), skunk goldenrod (*Solidago glomerata*) or galax. Quite often the smell will be emanating from a nearby stand of galax.

A note titled "Wild Ideas: The Odor of Galax" by J. Amoroso that appeared in *Chinquapin: The Newsletter of the Southern Appalachian Botanical Society* in 2000 reviewed speculations by several botanists about the possible causes for these odiferous emanations. A plant physiologist and chemist, working separately, have surmised that the smells might come from sulfur compounds similar to those exuded by skunks. Crushed living galax leaves produce no smell—but sulfur compounds could be released as the older leaves decompose.

Because its large shiny leaves assume beautiful colors in late fall—reds, bronzes, purples or browns—galax has been gathered commercially since the nineteenth century. Initially, entire families ventured into the mountains to collect them in burlap bags known as "tow sacks." They were then sold to botanical companies specializing in herbal medicines and ornamentals that marketed them as seasonal evergreen decorations. For the mountain families the few dollars earned were more than welcome.

Today, galax leaves are in high demand in the floral industry, both in America and Europe, because they are attractive, sturdy and can be stored for months. Rounded or heart-shaped leaves are preferred as background foliage in floral arrangements. They can also be hot-glued onto a plastic tray or wrapped to make a "floral rose." And they are sometimes sewn together to form tablecloths for weddings or blankets for funeral caskets.

As a sign of the times, upward of 90 percent of the galax pickers today are Hispanic. After these workers started arriving in the Blue Ridge during the late 1980s, area nursery owners encouraged them to harvest galax in the off-season. An experienced harvester can collect up to five thousand leaves a day and earn from $20 to $120, depending on the season and the size and color of the leaves. Concerns about the sustainability of galax have prompted the U.S. Forest Service to restrict both the quantity gathered and the harvest season. At this time, permits cost $25 and are good for thirty days or one hundred pounds of leaves, whichever comes first. Each leaf must be at least three inches in diameter, with three inches of stem and no roots attached.

Because of galax poaching on National Park Service lands such as the Great Smoky Mountains National Park, Shenandoah National Park and the Blue Ridge Parkway, as well as on U.S. Forest Service lands where harvesting is not allowed, a tagging program for the plant has been implemented. Leaves are sprayed with an adhesive and then dusted with a "micro-taggant"—a six-layer polymer that bears a "signature" coding. Using this method, plants in areas where harvesting is illegal are marked and can be traced back to their source when sold.

(A primary source for this essay was the excellent thirty-four-page pamphlet by Mary L. Predny and James L. Chamberlain, *Galax* (Galax urceolata): *An Annotated Bibliography*.)

9.

OIL NUT:

THAT MOST CURIOUS FRUIT

For Elizabeth and me, the fall season is one of the most invigorating times to get out in the woods and prowl around. Many of the most beautiful wildflowers found in the Blue Ridge, especially the lobelias and gentians, are then coming into their own. And most of the others are in their fruiting stages. Observing the transition from flower to fruit (or seed) is enjoyable. The varied fruiting forms—which run the gamut from drupes, berries and pomes, to follicles, utricles, loments and legumes, to capsules, achenes, samaras and nuts—are as attractive and intricate in their own way as any wildflower. And they are, after all, the grand finales of the germination-flowering-pollination cycle.

Some plants are more conspicuous in their flowering form, while others stand out when they produce fruit. The latter would include doll's-eyes, hearts-a-bustin' or strawberry bush, virgin's bower, sumac, carrion vine, pokeberry, sassafras, chinquapin, foxtail grass, wild oats, bittersweet, winterberry, American holly, mountain ash, ginseng, nightshade, wild yam and many others. A peculiar instance is oil nut (*Pyrularia pubera*), a fairly large shrub in the Sandalwood Family (*Santalaceae*) also known as buffalo nut, elk nut, tallow nut and rabbit wood. During every fall season, I have several people contact me to ask, "What is the name of that plant with the curious little green fruits that resemble pears?" Answer: oil nut.

In floodplains and upland woods, oil nut thrives in the mountains from Pennsylvania to Georgia and Alabama. It bears inconspicuous small greenish flowers from late April through May. The leaves are prominently veined, alternate, deciduous and lance-shaped, often being long-pointed at their tips. When it's not in fruit, I recognize the plant by the distinctive apple-green color of these leaves. It's the only species of the genus *Pyrularia* found in the western hemisphere—the other three being natives of southeastern Asia.

In late summer and fall, oil nut displays a pear-shaped fruit that's an eye-catcher. It contains a single round brownish nut about the size of a marble. The green exterior husk is mealy and oily, while the interior of the nut consists of meat about the color and consistency of that found inside an acorn.

The common names oil nut and tallow nut suggest that the fruit might provide a substance that would burn. And this is supported by S.B. Buckley, a botanist who roamed the Blue Ridge during the nineteenth century and wrote that the fruit is "so oily that it will burn like a candle if a wick be drawn through it."

In their essay "John Lyon, Nurseryman and Plant Hunter, and His Journal, 1799–1814" (1963), botanical historians Joesph and Nesta Ewan made some interesting observations about the botanical interest in oil nut during the nineteenth century:

> *William Hamilton, for whom Muhlenberg named the oil-nut* Hamiltonia oleifera, *and B.S. Barton were interested in the product, and perhaps Lyon may have hoped to find a large enough quantity to merchandise the nuts, which sometimes attain the size of a "musket ball." F.A. Michaux sought and found Pyrularia a short distance from West Liberty Town, near the plantation of Mr. Patrick Archibald in western Pennsylvania in July, 1802…Michaux describes how his father (Andre Michaux) had discovered the shrub fifteen years previously in the mountains of South Carolina, but had been unsuccessful in growing it in cultivation.*

In *Cherokee Plants: Their Uses—A 400 Year History* (1975), Paul B. Hamel and Mary C. Chiltoskey recorded that the early Cherokees called the plant "colic ball" in reference to the inner nut, which was chewed so as "to make vomit for [curing] colic." They also prepared a salve from the fruit that was reputed to cure "old sores."

Although oil nut quite obviously produces its own chlorophyll, it is partially parasitic, deriving water and minerals from the rootstock of several hosts in the plant communities where it grows, primarily various hardwood trees and shrubs. It has also been identified as a potential parasite on Fraser fir trees when they are grown at lower elevations so as to be sold as Christmas trees.

10.

HEPATICA:

"THE GEM OF THE WOODS"

NOTHING IS FAIRER, IF AS FAIR, AS THE FIRST FLOWER, THE HEPATICA. I FIND I HAVE NEVER ADMIRED THIS LITTLE FIRSTLING HALF ENOUGH. WHEN AT THE MATURITY OF ITS CHARMS, IT IS CERTAINLY THE GEM OF THE WOODS. WHAT AN INDIVIDUALITY IT HAS! NO TWO CLUSTERS ALIKE; ALL SHADES AND SIZES. A SOLITARY BLUE-PURPLE ONE, FULLY EXPANDED AND RISING OVER THE BROWN LEAVES OR THE GREEN MOSS, ITS CLUSTER OF MINUTE ANTHERS SHOWING LIKE A GROUP OF PALE STARS ON ITS LITTLE FIRMAMENT, IS ENOUGH TO ARREST AND HOLD THE DULLEST EYE.

—JOHN BURROUGHS, NINETEENTH-CENTURY NATURALIST

Contrary to Burroughs's observation, hepatica doesn't display the earliest flowers that bloom each year in the Blue Ridge. Those of bitter cress, henbit, purple dead nettle, bird's-eye speedwell and others appear in open, moist, sunny spots by late January or early February. But to my way of thinking, year in and year out, hepatica is the earliest of the truly showy woodland wildflowers. Trailing arbutus also has a reputation in this regard. One often reads of those who discover it blooming under late snows. But I hardly ever observe arbutus doing much more than budding before April.

Some botanical authorities maintain there is but one species of hepatica (*Hepatica noblis*) in North America. I concur, however, with those botanists—such as University of Tennessee botanist B. Eugene Wofford, author of *Guide to the Vascular Plants of the Blue Ridge* (1989)—who assert that there are two distinct species. Both are found in the Blue Ridge. The most common is sharp-lobed hepatica (*Hepatica acutiloba*). As its scientific and common names indicate, each leaf of this species displays three lobes that are sharply pointed. The less common species is round-lobed hepatica (*Hepatica americana*), which displays blunt leaf lobes.

As early as February, hepatica's three to eight flowering heads emerge on hairy stems that stand three to six inches high. These display petals, which might or might not be scented, can be white, pink, rose, lavender or a shimmering electric blue. Jack Sanders noted in *The Secret of Wildflowers: A Delightful Feast of Little-Known Facts, Folklore, and History* (2003) that "the hairy stems probably have two purposes: warmth and defense. They may also dissuade ants from climbing to the flowers and stealing the nectar."

Woodland flowers that appear very early each spring have the advantage of obtaining abundant sunlight before the leaf canopy closes overhead in late spring. They also have less competition for pollinating insects. A negative aspect of this strategy is that few potential pollinators are out in force so early—and hepatica is apparently not one of their favorites. Researchers have found that other early-flowering plants, such as trout lily, cut-leaved toothwort and wood anemone, tend to attract more bees and other insects. In order to hedge its bets, hepatica produces a percentage of flowers each year that are self-fertilized through a process botanists call "autogamy."

The generic designation *Hepatica* means, in Latin, "pertaining to the liver." This is a reference to the shape and color patterns of the second-year leaves, which—as botanist Jim Horton described them in *The Summer Times* (1979)—"have generally turned a rather lurid purplish brown and, being three-lobed, suggest the liver." Accordingly, the plant is often called liverleaf and serves as a textbook example of a concept known as the Doctrine of Signatures. Early plant collectors and herbalists putting this concept into practice took their lead from Paracelsus, the sixteenth-century Swiss physician who taught that God stamped each medicinally useful plant with a sign or signature that conveys to mankind the appropriate use to which the plant should be put. Numerous plant names—both scientific and common—are based on this idea.

The lobed and purplish-brown leaves of hepatica seemingly indicated to early botanists that the plant was "signed" for liver ailments. Jack Sanders recorded that during the nineteenth century hepatica treatments were all the rage—so much so, that in 1883 alone patent-medicine manufacturers used "more than 200 tons of hepatica leaves." Leaf extract administered to those suffering from "torpid liver" or "black bile" (*melan cholo*) no doubt induced more melancholy than it alleviated. It was even prescribed for kidney, bladder and lung ailments. Sal Hepatica ("liver salt") was at one time an enormously popular home remedy for constipation—but it just used the name, not the plant. And a brew made from hepatica leaves was even prescribed for those suffering from cowardice and freckles, as those two maladies were thought to be liver-related.

11.

THE SPRING
EPHEMERAL
STRATEGY

THERE IS A GROUP OF...WILDFLOWERS
CALLED SPRING EPHEMERALS. THEY
LIVE ON THE FOREST FLOOR BELOW THE
TOWERING DECIDUOUS CANOPIES OF
TEMPERATE NORTH AMERICA. THEY
ARE VERY BEAUTIFUL; BUT MORE THAN
BEAUTIFUL, THEY ARE VERY SPECIAL IN
THE TIME AND PLACE OF THEIR BEING.
THEY HAVE ZEROED IN ON A LIFESTYLE
WHICH IS DOWNRIGHT ENTERPRISING,
AND THEY LIVE BY A PRECISE SCHEDULE
THAT WOULD IMPRESS THE COMMUTER
WHO MUST MAKE AN 8:10 TRAIN EACH
MORNING.

—MICHAEL GODFREY, *A CLOSER LOOK* (1975)

The distinctive group of wildflowers categorized as spring ephemerals includes some of the more showy and renowned Blue Ridge species: white trout lily (*Erythronium albidum*), yellow adder's tongue (*E. americanum*), yellow trout lily

(*E. umbilicatum*), squirrel corn (*Dicentra canadensis*), Dutchman's-breeches (*D. cucullaria*), Virginia spring beauty (*Claytonia virginica*), Carolina spring beauty (*C. caroliniana*), cut-leaved toothwort (*Dentaria laciniata*) and wood anemone (*Anemone quinquefolia*). Peter White and the other authors of *Wildflowers of the Smokies* (1996) noted that ecologists "speak of a group of species with similar broad adaptations as a 'guild.'"

As the name indicates, members of the spring ephemeral guild are of short duration. Leafing out from underground storage tubers, corms, bulbs or fleshy rhizomes in rich deciduous woodlands, they flower quickly and are pollinated before the overarching trees have expanded their leaf buds overhead. Fruits ripen within weeks. Not long after the leaf canopy closes in late spring or early summer, the ephemerals will have died almost completely back, leaving little or no trace of their aboveground forms.

For the sake of clarity, I'll restate the spring ephemeral strategy. The plants in this group have high photosynthetic rates that allow them to rapidly accumulate carbohydrates and complete aboveground growth in a few weeks. Within a short span of time, they generate and store enough reserves to last until the following spring. Ephemerals have obviously adapted so as to take full advantage of the direct sunlight that's available before energy-giving light levels drop—at which time, they become essentially dormant rather than unnecessarily expending energy to maintain foliage. Peter White and his co-authors made the additional point that "if a plant leafs and flowers in different seasons then it has the problem of storing energy until flowering time, but if it does both at once, its leaves transfer energy-rich compounds directly to reproduction."

The designation spring ephemeral has at times been applied erroneously to other early-blooming woodland herbs such as bloodroot, Jack-in-the-pulpit, wild ginger, hepatica, woods phlox and the various trilliums. But these species don't qualify for the ephemeral guild because they retain leaves and ripen fruit well after the leaf canopy closes.

Slender fumewort (*Corydalis micrantha*) also has been cited as a spring ephemeral, but this plant doesn't qualify since it normally grows on sandy roadsides and in fields or waste places where its life cycle is not correlated with a woodland canopy sequence.

One advantage the ephemerals gain by flowering early is that they then have less competition from other plants for pollinating insects, primarily bumblebees, but also various sweat bees, flies and butterflies. Pollination of Dutchman's-breeches (the dainty little plant with blossom spurs that make it look for all the world like pantaloons hung out to dry) and the closely related squirrel corn can only be accomplished when a bumblebee forces apart the partially fused petal tips to sip nectar with their long tongues. A closer look will sometimes reveal that a flower has been "robbed" by shorter-tongued honeybees that bore holes in the tips of the spurs.

Early spring pollinators are frequently slowed in their search for food by cold, rainy or cloudy spells. In response, trout lilies have developed an ingenious backup system. To guard against an absence of pollinators, trout lily plants can reproduce asexually via a fleshy bud (dropper) that forms at the end of a fragile white stem (stolon) attached to the base of the parent corm. This dropper stem can be as long as ten inches. Dense colonies that form along creek banks are for the most part created from droppers rather than seed. Missouri Botanical Garden botanist Peter Bernhardt—author of *Wily Orchids & Underground Orchids: Revelations of a Botanist* (1989)—calculated that as much as 90 percent of all the trout lily species native to eastern North America are reproduced asexually.

When you happen upon a trout lily colony in early spring, note that the plants in bloom will all have two leaves. Botanists disagree as to whether the clones produced by droppers ever develop two leaves and flower, or whether only the seed-produced individuals flower. Be that as it may, individual flowers take up to eight years to reach reproductive maturity. The yellow petals (actually "tepals"—an undifferentiated form between a sepal and a petal) are at first partially closed.

Gradually, these reflex so as to fully expose the interior parts of the flower to pollinators.

Ephemerals need to be able to store food efficiently. Squirrel corn, for instance, has bright yellow nutrient-storage bulbs attached to its root system that resemble corn kernels. You can readily observe them without harming the plant by gently scraping back the leaf litter. Squirrels are reputed to harvest and store these bulbs in food caches; if so, they may inadvertently help distribute the plant.

In regard to ephemeral distribution tactics, Peter White and the co-authors of *Wildflowers of the Smokies* (1996) made this acute observation: "There is another reason to fruit in spring. Many ephemerals are ant dispersed. They have special adaptations to attract ants that carry their seeds to new places, even planting them in or on the mineral soil. Often the seeds carry a special oily body that is especially attractive to ants. Spring seems to be a good time to be ant dispersed." And in *The Secret of Wildflowers: A Delightful Feast of Little-Known Facts, Folklore, and History* (2003), Jack Sanders provided additional background:

> *Some species of ants harvest and "plant"...certain other spring wildflowers in a symbiotic relationship called myrmecochory—literally "ant farming." They are drawn to the seeds by small protuberances...that contain attractive oils and possibly sugars. The ants carry the seeds, sometimes as far as 70 yards, to their nests where they eat the treat. The shell, however, is too hard to open, so the ants discard the seed proper, often in an unused tunnel in the nest. Here, amid nutrients provided by the soil and accidentally by the housekeeping ants, the seed has a much better chance of producing a plant than one does dropped on the forest floor where it may be eaten by foraging birds and rodents.*

Complex adjustments of this sort by a guild of flowering plants to the canopy development of an upland deciduous forest—as well as to the needs of its animal residents—were no doubt formed through a long period of coexistence. For me, this exemplifies a collective life, of sorts, whereby a community of animals and plants lives in harmony with a particular landscape.

12

PLANT TRAPS:

BY DEVIOUS MEANS

Whe teaching plant identification workshops, I always remind participants that the pleasures we get from observing the beauty of flowers or the elegance of fruiting structures arise from the basic utilitarian objectives of plants. Everything about a flower—color, shape or fragrance—is there to attract pollinators and produce a fruit of some sort. In turn, everything about a fruiting structure—those that are carried by the wind, float or are eaten by animals—has to do with seed distribution. It's that simple. Plant beauty is a byproduct of form following function in a manner that is often exquisite.

It's fascinating to observe the strategies plants have developed to accomplish these ends. One that particularly interests me is displayed by those species that trap insects to enhance their possibilities for pollination. I'm not referring to the various carnivorous plants like pitcher plants, sundews and bladderworts. These capture insects for food, not pollination. They do so with non-floral parts—either specially adapted leaves or underwater siphoning devices—that enable them to dissolve the insects and convert their proteins into nitrogen. But there are two very common Blue Ridge plants with highly unusual flowers that imprison insects for pollination purposes. One does so for the short term, the other for life.

Dutchman's pipe (*Aristolochia macrophylla*) is a grayish rope-like vine that can be up to four inches in diameter. In rich upland forests up to five thousand feet in elevation, it can climb to one hundred feet into the canopy of large trees. It's the only twining vine in our woodlands with clusters of short twigs along the main stem. The large valentine-shaped leaves, which can be ten or more inches wide, are a visual clue for locating this plant. May is its usual month for flowering.

The flowers have been described as being "S-shaped," "shaped like a saxophone" or resembling "the large-bowled pipes traditionally smoked by the burghers of the Netherlands." The curved body of the "pipe" and the base of the "bowl" are purplish-brown. The flat top of the "bowl" is yellowish and three-lobed. In its center is a hole that provides an entryway for small insects like gnats and flies, which are attracted by a carrion-like odor. Because this entrance is lined with stiff hairs that point inward, the insect gets trapped. The hollow chamber within the flower bends downward and then upward. The male stamens and female pistil are situated at the farther, upturned end of the "pipe"— where the insect-rewarding nectar is also deposited.

Herbert Waldron Faulkner first described what happens in *The Mysteries of the Flowers* (1917). The pistil is the first to ripen, so that an intruding insect can quickly deposit pollen brought from another flower. But the insect is not allowed to escape until, in due time, the anthers ripen and shed their pollen on the trapped critter. The flower tube then withers and hangs limply down so that the hairs no long restrain the insect, allowing it to escape and visit another Dutchman's pipe flower. The cross-fertilization process is thereby continued from plant to plant. Faulkner didn't, however, make the additional point that insects not carrying pollen when they enter a flower will be trapped until an insect arrives with pollen to trigger the release mechanism.

Successfully pollinated flowers develop pendant cucumber-like fruits in late summer and fall that are three to six inches long and green in color. These ripen and split to expose stacks of winged seeds that the autumn winds disperse.

Another familiar plant of the mountain region that traps insects for the same reason is Jack-in-the-pulpit, which is every bit as curious in its floral architecture. Indeed, Jack-in-the-pulpit outdoes the convoluted shenanigans of Dutchman's pipe in that it has plants that are either male or female, which can—if need be—change sexes from year to year.

In spring and early summer, Jack-in-the-pulpits appear in rich woodlands as a plant bearing either one or two long-stalked leaves with three large leaflets each. These can range from small pale plants a few inches high to thick-stemmed, dark-mottled individuals over three feet in height. The tubular hooded flowers (spathes) also vary in size and color from plant to plant. Through the years, some botanical authorities have attempted to recognize three or more distinct species, but most current manuals—including B. Eugene Wofford's *Guide to the Vascular Plants of the Blue Ridge* (1989)—list but a single species: *Arisaema triphyllum*.

Another common name is Indian turnip because the roots are shaped something like a turnip. Cherokees and other American Indians roasted them to make a starchy powder and bread-like food. Before doing so, however, they had to let the rootstock dry for at least six months. This aging neutralized the effects of the needle-like crystals of calcium oxalate fresh plants contain. When eaten fresh, these crystals pierce the mouth, throat and stomach lining, causing what has been described as "a fiery hot acidity."

Jack Sanders depicted Jack-in-the-pulpits as "one of our strangest-looking flowering plants" in *The Secret of Wildflowers* (2003):

The common name is perfect. The long spathe looks like an old-fashioned pulpit, complete with overhead baffle to reflect and spread sermons throughout the church in the days before public address systems. For the plant, however, the hood is simply an umbrella, preventing the vertical, tube-like spathe from filling with rainwater…"Jack" is the spadix, the club-like, flower-bearing stick that stands erect in the pulpit with just his head protruding to survey his "congregation." Jack has long been a common colloquialism for "fellow" or "guy"…The plant is so constructed and colored that insects, especially fungus gnats, are drawn down the spathe to the base of the spadix, which bears the tiny flowers. The floor of a chamber at the base of the tube is covered with pollen. After it has descended and picked up the pollen, an insect has a hard time leaving. It cannot easily climb back up the slippery tube, nor up the spadix because of a projecting ledge. The only exit is a small flap at the base, where the two sides of the pulpit join. Insects that are small or strong enough can find and squeeze through this "door" to move onto other plants.

In March 1982, biologist Paulette Bierzychudek published an article in *Natural History Magazine* titled "Jack and Jill in the Pulpit" that caught my eye. So much so, that I have been paying close attention to the plant ever since. Based on her research, Bierzychudek explained that during each growing season a Jack-in-the-pulpit produces tiny flowers at the base of the spadix that are either male (a cluster of creamy white or purplish anthers) or female (green spherical structures capable of producing seeds).

A plant without large rootstock and excess food supplies will bear one-leaved plants that are male. Rootstock that is large with lots of stored food produces two-leaved plants that are female. Females require this sort of energy surplus to produce the large cluster of red berries that develop on the spadix in the fall. If, for whatever reason, the energy stores of a female plant decline, it can become a one-leaved male flower capable of producing pollen or even revert to being a plant without a flower that is neither male nor female. Conversely, a male that develops its storage supplies can produce two leaves, change sexes and become a seed-bearing female. Via this uncanny system of sexual flexibility, Jack-in-the-pulpit plants can make the best possible response to changing environmental factors.

I had my doubts after reading Bierzychudek's findings, but whenever I take a peek inside a Jack-in-the-pulpit spathe her conclusions are verified about 90 percent of the time: one-leaved plants will be male, and two-leaved plants will be female. If you, too, start stooping to check on these plants, notice that when there are male flowers at the base of the spadix there will be a tiny hole (described above by Sanders as a "door") at the base of the spathe. This exit allows the insect to escape bearing

pollen and visit a nearby female plant. But you will also notice that there is no escape hole at the base of a female spathe. Thereby, the devious "Jill"-in-the-pulpit traps the insect, forcing it to fly around and around seeking a way out. The chances of pollination taking place are thereby enhanced exponentially. But for the insect—which almost never escapes through the entrance at the top of the spathe—its imprisonment is a death sentence.

When female spathes are dissected, dead insects can often be observed at the base of the closed chambers. There is no firm evidence that female plants absorb nutrients from these insects. But as Jack Sanders also observed: "The bottoms of the pulpits often contain insect corpses, leading some scientific observers to wonder whether the Jack-in-the-pulpit is evolving slowly over the eons into an insect-eating variety like the pitcher plant or Venus flytrap."

(Additional sources regarding Jack-in-the-pulpit's sex-reversal and insect-catching strategies are George Constantz, *Hollows, Peepers, and Highlanders*; Stephen Jay Gould, *The Flamingo's Smile*; and Harold N. Moldenke, *American Wildflowers*.)

13.

CHEROKEE BASKETS:
SPLINTS AND DYES

WOVEN GOODS—BASKETS AND MATS—
DOCUMENT WHAT WOMEN DID, WHEN,
AND HOW. THEY ILLUMINATE THE
WORK OF WOMEN WHO TRANSFORMED
THE ENVIRONMENTS THAT PRODUCED
MATERIALS FOR BASKETRY. THEY POINT
TO WOMEN'S ROLES IN CEREMONIAL,
SUBSISTENCE, AND EXCHANGE SYSTEMS.
AS OBJECTS CREATED AND UTILIZED BY
WOMEN, BASKETS AND MATS CONSERVED
AND CONVEYED THEIR CONCEPTS, IDEAS,
EXPERIENCE, AND EXPERTISE. THEY
ASSERTED WOMEN'S CULTURAL IDENTITY
AND REFLECTED THEIR VALUES.
—SARAH H. HILL, *WEAVING NEW WORLDS:*
SOUTHEASTERN CHEROKEE WOMEN AND THEIR
BASKETRY (1997)

I don't know of an adult Cherokee man or woman who is
not a craftsperson of one sort or another. It's an amazing
culture in many ways, but they are particularly distinguished
in regard to stone and woodcarvings, basketry, jewelry, pottery
and similar crafts. In this era of casino gambling and economic

revitalization, it will be interesting to observe how members of the Eastern Band of Cherokee Indians maintain these traditions, especially basket making—the one for which they are perhaps most famed. As a naturalist, I have been particularly interested in the materials they harvested and processed to make splints and dyes.

I've seen photos made in the late nineteenth century of entire families canoeing along rivers in western North Carolina to gather river cane (*Arundinaria gigantean*). Until the early twentieth century, sizable canebrakes existed in the flatlands alongside many of the larger waterways in the Blue Ridge. Ironically, modern Cherokees—longstanding masters of cane implementation—are having to venture to areas outside the mountains to find suitable cane for their baskets, mats, flutes and other items.

For some time, it was my assumption that the Cherokees had used white oak (*Quercus alba*) as a source for basket splints since emerging as a distinctive culture a thousand or so years ago. Through Sarah Hill's fine book, however, I learned that the European settlers introduced the Cherokees to the concept of using white oak. Hill's research indicated that, "even though Cherokees and whites lived in close proximity and traded with each other for two centuries before the removal (1838), no evidence indicates that Cherokee weavers fully incorporated white oak into their basketry traditions prior to the nineteenth century."

She noted that river cane can be harvested any time of the year and is then soaked in a stream to keep it fresh. Preparation includes trimming the leaves, smoothing rough joints and splitting each stalk into four to eight sticks. An expert "can split a stalk in less than five minutes." The trickiest part comes when the outer cortex of the stick is painstakingly separated from the inner core with a knife. If this procedure is successful, the process yields a thin, pliable section of inner core called a splint. Hill's description of the basket maker absorbed in her work is captivating:

Around her feet, long segments of discarded cores pile up, filling the air with a fresh, pungent odor. The work continues hour after hour, the rhythmic strokes of the weaver's hands keeping time with the sounds of the splitting cane.

Next the inner side of each splint is tediously scraped again and again to remove all of the pith fibers. The prepared splints are rolled into circular bundles that are secured with ties. They are ready for the dying process.

The Cherokees are dye masters. They can obtain the exact shades desired by manipulating various factors: the amount of pulp, the source of the pulp (root, bark, leaf or husk) and the amount of time splints were left in a boiling cauldron of water. Mordants are reactive agents used to fix or set coloring matter in textiles, leather, basket splints and other materials. Hill reported that Cherokee weavers "may use soda, alum, or copper as a mordant. Some remember that their mothers added old iron froes, ax heads, or nails to walnut dye pots." Several Cherokee basket makers have told me that ashes and urine were also used.

Hill mentioned a number of Cherokee dye sources, but in my experience they have traditionally favored four plants: bloodroot (*Sanguinaria canadensis*) for orange-red; black walnut (*Juglans nigra*) for brown; butternut walnut (*Juglans cinerea*) for black; and shrub yellowroot (*Xanthorhiza simplicissima*) for yellow. Pulped rootstock was always used from shrub yellowroot and bloodroot. To avoid killing the walnut trees, the bark or hulls were often used instead of rootstock.

Bloodroot is one of the most attractive spring-blooming wildflowers in the eastern United States. The first part of its scientific name means "bleeding"—a reference to the peculiar red fluid that oozes from the rootstock when broken. Other members of the Poppy Family also produce this acrid fluid, which contains various alkaloids.

Black walnut is common in disturbed areas throughout the lower elevations of the Blue Ridge. Because of an invasive fungus, butternut walnut—also called white walnut—is becoming increasingly difficult to locate.

It's relatively easy to distinguish the smaller butternut walnut from its larger cousin. Each butternut leaf has a large terminal leaflet, whereas black walnut has either a smallish terminal leaflet or no terminal leaflet at all. The bark of a mature butternut walnut is gray to light brown, being divided into deep furrows that form a characteristic diamond-shaped pattern. Butternut leaves and fruit drop early revealing conspicuous, three-lobed (inversely triangular) leaf scars on twigs, each of which is surrounded by a raised, downy, gray pad or "eyebrow." Botanical manuals often describe these scars as looking "like a ram's face."

Shrub yellowroot grows profusely along numerous creeks throughout the Blue Ridge. It's a plant up to twenty inches in height that resembles a tiny palm tree because all of the leafy green growth is at the top of stem. The purplish-brown flowers appear as early as February on graceful drooping racemes about three inches in length.

Some years ago I interviewed Martha Ross, a resident of the Big Cove Community on the Qualla Boundary (Cherokee). She and her three sisters—Maggie Lossiah, Jane Taylor and Dorothy Thompson—all learned basket making from their mother, Charlotte Lossiah. "Mother didn't use yellowroot as a dye too much except with honeysuckle," Mrs. Ross recalled.

> *She liked to use bloodroot. But I like yellowroot. We also use butternut and walnut.*
>
> *You can gather yellowroot anytime, but it's best in spring when you get a brighter color. It's a little dull in winter. The roots can be used if you beat them with a hammer, but I like the stems to get the prettiest yellow.*
>
> *You scrape the pulp into a kettle of boiling water on the stove. Pull the splints out to the edge so that the yellow fills up a little hole in the center. After thirty or forty minutes it's ready. I never dye a big batch at once, just enough to make a few baskets.*

Hopefully, current and future generations of Cherokee artisans will be as interested as Martha Ross was in listening, observing and maintaining the old ways of doing things. If so, assistance will be available from the Revitalization of Traditional Cherokee Artisan Resources program, whose stated purpose is "to assist the Eastern Band of Cherokee Indians as the tribe works to restore the traditional Cherokee balance between maintaining and using natural resources like river cane, white oak and clay."

The program is funded by the Cherokee Preservation Foundation and operated through the Cherokee Studies program at Western Carolina University. Recent initiatives include contracting with the University of Tennessee to plant one thousand butternut seedlings on property owned by the Eastern Band and plans for establishing a River Cane Research Station in western North Carolina to determine ideal conditions for establishing and sustaining canebrakes. The program's website is provided in my list of sources.

14.

WINTER ORCHIDS:

PUTTYROOT AND

CRANEFLY ORCHIS

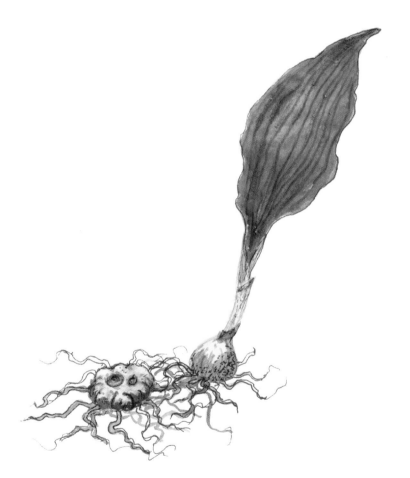

In the Blue Ridge there are about fifty native orchid species. We think of showy orchis and lady's-slippers in spring, yellow- and purple-fringed orchids in summer and ladies'-tresses in autumn. But as curious as it may seem, winter is the prime time to locate and identify several of our native orchid species, using their distinctive leaves.

The solitary basal leaves of puttyroot (*Aplectrum hymale*) and cranefly orchis (*Tipularia discolor*) emerge in late summer, after the flowering period, and are conspicuous in rich, rocky woodlands from late November into early spring. Then, as the flowering stems emerge in spring, the leaves wither and disappear. For this reason, they are sometimes called winter leaf or hibernal orchids, but I think of them as "winter orchids."

This winter leaf strategy obviously evolved as an efficient way to collect the sun's energy in rich hardwood forests when the leaf canopy is absent. Both plants have prominent bulb-shaped roots (corms) that are well adapted for energy storage. Once the canopy closes overhead in spring, the leaves die back to allow the energy to be channeled directly into flowering and fruiting processes.

Cranefly orchis derived its common name from the fancied resemblance of its delicate flowers to the insect of that name.

Although the plant is rather common throughout the Blue Ridge, it is inconspicuous when flowering. The winter leaf is its outstanding feature. The upper side is dark green and purple spotted with wart-like bumps, so that, in some ways, it resembles a toad's back. The underside is a rich satiny purple.

There are only two species of *Tipularia* in the world. The other is found in the Himalayas. Studies indicate that cranefly orchis germinates on decomposing wood from a variety of tree species. Each plant stem can stand up to two feet tall and bear as many as twenty blossoms whose delicate threadlike parts resemble a swarm of purplish insects.

By assuming this devious appearance, the plant is able to attract the pollinators it requires to accomplish fertilization.

Puttyroot, also called Adam-and-Eve root, is my favorite of the two winter orchid species. It is quite common throughout the Blue Ridge. The attractive gray-green oval leaf can grow up to seven inches long by three inches wide. As described by Douglas B. Elliott in *Roots: An Underground Botany and Forager's Guide* (1976), "This leaf has thin, white pinstripes, is folded like a pleated skirt, green on the top side, with a tinge of purple underneath."

One of puttyroot's common names comes from a mucilaginous fluid that can be extracted from the tubers when crushed. Numerous sources report that the early white settlers made a paste from this fluid that was used to mend broken crockery and other items. But long before their arrival on the scene, the Cherokees, according to Paul B. Hamel and Mary U. Chiltoskey in *Cherokee Plants and Their Uses* (1975), had discovered the high-energy content of this rootstock and fed it to their babies so as to make them fleshy and fat. For some unknown reason, the Cherokees also believed that consuming this fare would enable their babies to grow up to be eloquent orators.

The other common name, Adam-and-Eve root, is derived from the fact that this year's leaf-bearing corm (Eve) remains attached to last year's corm (Adam) by a strand (stolon) of umbilical-like root filament. Elliott asserted that the root system has "a cupid-like reputation for helping to maintain the bond between lovers [who] each receive one of the corms…As the legend goes, so long as the pair maintains possession of their respective roots, their bond shall remain strong and true."

15

FIDDLEHEADS AND FERNS THAT WALK

Plants classified within the botanical division *Pteridophyta* are known as *Pteridophytes* (ta-rid-o-phytes). In addition to ferns, this division includes the so-called "fern allies": horsetails, scouring rushes, quillworts, spikemosses and club mosses. Ferns are our most graceful plants. They are things of beauty, providing varied forms that delight the eye and add harmony to any woodland landscape. Henry David Thoreau said it best: "God created ferns to show what he could do with leaves."

Even those not especially interested in ferns have heard of fiddleheads and know that they're supposedly edible. Whenever I'm conducting a fern identification workshop, someone almost always asks: "Where can I find a fiddlehead fern?" I know right away the person thinks there is a fern species named "fiddlehead" and that their prime interest is the possibility of eating some. My response is that fiddleheads aren't a fern species but a growth form. That is, all ferns display some sort of fiddlehead-like shape when they arise from the plant's underground rhizomes—and a number of species display growth tips that closely resemble the shape carved at the head of a fiddle.

A "fern leaf" (frond) differs from the "true leaf" of a flowering plant in how it expands from the bud. With ferns, the leaf unrolls from the tip rather than opening from a folded condition. This unfurling strategy helps the immature frond make its way upward through soil and leaf litter. It also protects the developing leaflets (pinna) that will make up the leafy portion (blade) of the mature frond. The first fronds that appear in a new season are purely vegetative—those unfurling later produce the spores by which ferns propagate.

The technical name for a fiddlehead is "crozier." This is derived from the name for the crooked end of a bishop's staff. These have a curved top symbolic of the Good Shepherd and are carried by officials of the Roman Catholic, Anglican and some European Lutheran churches as a symbol of their ecclesiastical office.

In addition to being highly functional, emerging fiddleheads of some fern species are quite beautiful. Those of cinnamon fern (*Osmunda cinnamomea*) are pale lime green and can stand a foot or more tall before unfurling. Species in the wood fern genus (*Dryopteris*) often display wooly greenish-brown fiddleheads.

Ostrich fern (*Matteuccia struthiopteris*), the species bearing fiddleheads reputed to be the most delicious in North America, doesn't grow wild in the Blue Ridge, as its range is more northern. Few of the ferns native to the southeastern portion of North America are considered by connoisseurs to be palatable. Bracken (*Pteridium aquilinum*)—which does grow in the Blue Ridge and is thought by some to be tasty—displays exquisite silvery-gray fiddleheads shaped like an eagle's claw. It is distributed worldwide, being found along roadsides and in disturbed areas with poor soil. But scientific research indicates bracken contains a number of toxic substances that kill livestock and might cause stomach cancers in human populations—as in Japan and China—where substantial amounts of the plant's rootstock or fiddleheads are eaten.

There are seventy or so fern species found in the Blue Ridge. That's not an overwhelming number, but even people with considerable knowledge of flowering plants tend to be intimidated by fern identification. They think it's too technical. This is wrong. Some ferns can be tricky, but anyone can learn to identify them with a little effort. Indeed, some of the more common species are so distinctive that one could learn to identify them in a single day. Cinnamon, interrupted, royal, rockcap, resurrection, northern maidenhair, bracken, ebony spleenwort, walking, sensitive, broad (or winged) beech, New York and Christmas ferns would all fall into that category.

As a non-technical identification key-guide for use in my fern workshops, I recommend *Fern Finder: A Guide to Native Ferns of Central and Northeastern United States and Eastern Canada* (2001) by Anne C. and Barbara G. Hallowell. This includes almost all of the fern species found in the Blue Ridge. I supplement the Hallowell key-guide with two other sources: Lloyd H. Snyder Jr. and James G. Bruce's *Field Guide to the Ferns and Other* Pteridophytes *of Georgia* (1986), which has excellent line drawings; and Murray Evans's *Ferns & Fern Allies of the Smokies* (2005), which features excellent photographs.

My favorite fern is walking fern (*Asplenium rhizophyllum*), which grows primarily in moss mats that form atop limestone boulders. It is unlike any other fern. One of the characteristics of plants is that, unlike animals, they're supposed to be immobile. But walking fern moves around anyway. It has the ability to root at the tips of its vegetative leaves and form new plants a short distance from the "parent" plant. Through the years, this fern will often create a circle around the original plant, giving the appearance of having moved or "walked."

16

CHEROKEE MUSHROOMS:
SLICKS, MILKYS AND WISHYS

T he humid forests and valleys of the Blue Ridge are renowned for their variety of mushrooms. To some, mushrooms seem spectral and fantastic—something out of a dream world, best avoided. To others, they represent adventure—objects to be sought out, identified and understood for their own intrinsic beauty and place in the ecological cycle. Then there are those who pursue them as delicacies—food items that wind up in gourmet dishes.

In the late 1980s, Elizabeth and I enrolled in a Smoky Mountain Field School course conducted by Ron Peterson, then the mycologist at the University of Tennessee. Doing so provided us with the rudimentary skills required to make accurate identifications of wild mushrooms. There are now twenty or so species that we harvest for the table, mainly in late summer and fall, which is the time of mushroom abundance. These include morels (a spring species), eastern cauliflower, sulphur shelf, hedgehog, chanterelle, horn of plenty, painted suillus, voluminous-latex lactarius, indigo lactarius, corrugated-cap lactarius, orange-latex lactarius, velvet foot, honey and oyster mushrooms.

We never take a chance with any species that's in a genus where poisonous species are found. Misidentifying a bird or a wildflower isn't a big deal, but misidentifying a mushroom that you're going to eat can be a really big deal—like death.

When I was growing up, my family never made reference to "mushrooms." In that time, people invariably called them "toadstools"—a negative label that implied they were suspect and not to be fooled with any more than true toads were to be handled because they gave you warts. But many of the earliest European settlers in North America (including my ancestors) came to this continent with a long-standing tradition of harvesting mushrooms. They immediately began harvesting, cooking and eating North American species that resembled the ones they had been fond of eating in the Old World. Trouble was that not a few of these proved to be deadly look-alikes.

That situation pretty much cured most of our early ancestors from having anything to do with "toadstools." On the west coast, the look-alike scenario is being replayed in the twenty-first century as modern immigrants from Asia make deadly mistakes when they harvest and ingest species that closely resemble ones that had been choice edibles in their homelands. Some of the eastern European immigrants to North America, however, have continued to harvest and ingest North American species to this day with success based on close observation and care.

It's interesting from a cultural viewpoint to note that the Indian peoples of both North and South America brought with them to the New World—supposedly from northeastern Asia—a great tradition of harvesting and ingesting mushrooms that has been continued to this day. One supposes they have done so by trial and error. That is, the American Indians no doubt made deadly identification errors, as did the Europeans, but they apparently recorded those errors in their oral traditions and tended not to repeat them.

If you take a basketful of recently harvested mushrooms into a barbershop in Cherokee, North Carolina, a lively discussion about what they are and where they were found will start. The Cherokees have their own names for each species and they know exactly the type of habitat in which each is found.

Armillariella mella is known to the Cherokees as "slicks" and to non-Indians as the honey mushroom. According to Cherokee native Amy Walker, an avid mushroom collector I spoke with some years ago, her people call them slicks because they "just slide right down your throat." This is true. Once the cap of a slick is heated, it becomes viscous and does indeed slide down your throat, one after the other, just like oysters. Walker noted that the Cherokees have traditionally harvested "milkys" (species in the *Lactarius* genus, all of which exude a milky fluid when cut or broken), "wishys" (apparently the species *Grifola frondosa*, known to non-Indians as "hen of the woods") and several others.

17.

WHITE SNAKEROOT:

THE MILK SICK STORY

Milk Sick Cove, Milk Sick Holler, Milk Sick Ridge, Milk Sick Knob and similar place names are common throughout the Blue Ridge. They are so-named because of an association with a once mysterious and deadly disease known variously as milk sick, milk sickness, puke fever, "the slows" or "the trembles."

White snakeroot (*Ageratina altissima* or *Eupatorium rugosum*), a close relative of joe-pye weed and white boneset, grows in profusion in the middle and upper elevations of the southern mountains, especially the Blue Ridge, and westward into the Mississippi Valley. It was scientifically identified during the first half of the twentieth century—after more than one hundred years of speculation—as the cause of milk sickness, when it was officially recognized that drinking the milk from cows that had eaten the plant often resulted in human fatalities, especially when consumed by infants.

The common name, white snakeroot, is derived from the color of the flowers and the occasional practice of using its rootstock to prepare a poultice for snakebites. As a general rule, however, the American Indians and white settlers didn't pay much attention to the fall-blooming, white-flowered plant with heart-shaped, rough-toothed and long-stemmed leaves.

From late summer into fall, mountaineers drove their cattle into the middle and higher elevations to graze. To this day along highland trails, one literally wades through profuse stands of white snakeroot for miles. But the cattle drovers never thought to associate the plant with milk sickness. Various authorities attributed the sickness to "a poisonous dew on the grass," razorback hogs, a non-existent "milk sick fly," toxic gases, poisonous minerals and so on, ad infinitum.

Even as late as 1914, when John Preston Arthur published his reliable *Western North Carolina: A History From 1730 to 1913*, the cause of milk sickness was not widely known outside of isolated areas in Ohio and Illinois. "This sickness is usually fatal to the victim unless properly treated," Arthur noted, while pointing out that the only remedy then known was to fence off the patch of land on which the cows had grazed. "There were, and still are, for that matter, men and women peculiarly skilled and successful in the treatment of this obscure disease, who were called 'milk sick' doctors. Sometimes they were not doctors or physicians at all, and did not pretend to practice medicine generally, seeming to know how to treat nothing except 'milk sick.' Whiskey or brandy with honey is the usual remedy; but, in the doses and proportionate parts of each ingredient and when to administer, it consisted of the skill of the physician."

I've been interested in and have written about milk sickness for many years. Here, then, is "The Milk Sick Story" as I presently understand it.

The search for the killer plant was filled with wrong turns, chauvinism, regionalism and pigheadedness. During the nineteenth century, scientific research was concentrated in the northeastern United States, where milk sickness did not occur. Accordingly, the problem was viewed from a theoretical perspective rather than from a practical and preventative one.

During the winter of 1816, a pioneer family ferried their meager possessions across the Ohio River and settled near Pigeon Creek, close to what is now Gentryville, Indiana. Thomas Lincoln built a crude, three-sided shelter that served as home until he could build a log cabin. In 1818, an epidemic of milk sick broke out. One of the first victims was Thomas's wife, Nancy Hanks Lincoln. As her son, Abraham, subsequently recorded, she died October 5, 1818.

In 1838 an Ohio farmer, suspecting that white snakeroot might be the cause, fed leaves from the plant to some of his animals. Sure enough, they developed milk sickness and died. The farmer published his exciting find in the local newspaper. But at that time, simple farmers couldn't make medical discoveries, could they? Nope, at that time, only the discoveries of certified (predominantly male) professionals were recognized or even considered. A famous eastern physician, Dr. Daniel Drake, denounced the farmer's experiments. Drake was convinced that the cause was poison ivy.

At about the same time, Anna Pierce Hobbs Bixby came into the Illinois wilderness with her family. Upset by the poor health of her neighbors, she decided to become a physician, as it were, and returned to Philadelphia to take courses in nursing, midwifery and dental extraction, which were the only courses offered to women at that time.

After her return to Illinois, an epidemic of milk sick raged in the little settlement where Doctor Anna now lived. She noted in her diary that the humans and animals contracting the disease had all been drinking milk. In an attempt to locate the "guilty" plant, she followed grazing cattle, observing the plants they fed upon. But Doctor Anna was baffled in her field research until she happened upon an elderly Indian medicine woman known as Aunt Shawnee. When Doctor Anna described what she was looking for to Aunt Shawnee, the older woman nodded, led her into the woods, and pointed to white snakeroot.

Like the Ohio farmer, Doctor Anna tested the plant on a calf, which soon developed "the trembles," while other animals not fed white snakeroot were fine. Accordingly, she started a white snakeroot eradication program that within three years virtually eliminated milk sickness from southeastern Illinois. Wanting other practitioners to know about white snakeroot, she grew a patch in her garden and wrote letters inviting physicians to come and examine it for themselves. But the eastern medical establishment ignored her findings as they had those of the Ohio farmer, setting back research and treatment for nearly a century and, indirectly, causing thousands upon thousands of deaths, predominantly among infants.

Finally, in the 1920s, researchers at the U.S. Department of Agriculture isolated from white snakeroot a highly complex alcohol they named tremetol. More resent research has refined the original USDA scientific analysis, but the culprit plant had, finally, been officially "discovered." Information was spread in the late 1920s throughout the medical and agricultural communities. Fencing laws and supervised milk treatment largely solved the milk sick problem.

But the memory of its devastating effects lives on in family genealogies, records kept in Bibles and rural cemeteries. In an article published in 2002 in the *Graham* (NC) *Star*, longtime U.S. Forest Service ranger Marshall McClung described a remote cemetery near Robbinsville in Graham County in western North Carolina, where the graves "were originally marked by small stones which gave no names or dates." More recently, according to McClung, someone erected a collective marker that reads: "Mostly Infants Who Died of the Milk Sick Before 1916."

III: Fauna

1.

Bird Lore

The superstitions of the folk of any country are not only interesting with thought, feeling, and belief... but through them much of the inner history of a people can often be traced.
—"Bird Superstitions and Winged Portents" (1898)

The bird lore and superstitions associated with the ancient Cherokees, pioneer settlers and their descendants in the Blue Ridge are always interesting and sometimes illuminating. It's challenging to try to detect "the inner history" of these materials. The Cherokees were our first ornithologists. Many of their legends are concerned with birds, and their sacred formulas (poems, songs and chants) constantly evoked them for various purposes. The pioneer settlers and their descendants didn't fail to record their bird impressions and anecdotes, either. Through the years, I have been collecting and writing about this body of lore. Here are some examples.

The blue jay is a noisy, showy and common bird that everyone recognizes. Many people have observed flocks of jays raiding nests in late spring, devouring both eggs and baby birds. It's distressing to hear the anguished calls of the parent birds as they try to defend their nests, for the most part unsuccessfully.

It's not surprising, then, that a considerable amount of negative lore has accumulated in regard to the blue jay. In an essay titled "Encyclopedia of Superstitions" that appeared in *My Mountains, My People* (1957), John Parris summarized these attitudes and beliefs:

> *The old man is an encyclopedia of superstitions. He carries a buckeye to ward off rheumatism and totes around a pinch of salt in his coat pocket—the left one—for good luck. He is a careful man and he has a keen eye for all the signs, albeit he is just three years shy of a hundred. Sometimes he will talk willingly about his beliefs and about good luck charms and superstitions. But these are rare occasions. When he does break over, however, he lights up his pipe, grins a bit and tells you that a-body's got to know the signs and go by 'em if he expects to get along.*
>
> *"Now, take the jay bird," he says. "That's a bird that's been known to be a sign of bad luck as long as I can remember. When I was a boy the old folks told me the jay once sold himself to the devil for a grain of corn. Ever since then the entire jay bird tribe has been paying off the debt by carrying sticks and sand to the devil every Saturday.*
>
> *"I don't want nothin' to do with a jay bird. It's a bird of the devil. Nothin' but trouble. They start comin' in just as soon as spring things start to growin' and start their devilment."*
>
> *Other old timers consider that the jay bird is a reporter for the devil and that he makes regular trips to hell carrying a list of the sins of people.*
>
> *Others say the jay makes a visit to hell only on Fridays to take some kindling, a drop of water or a grain of sand to the devil. Some say this grain of sand is part of a ransom for the souls waiting there who cannot be released until all sand visible on the surface of the earth has been carried below.*

The gist of these superstitions is clear enough. But why blue jays? Ravens, owls and even crows would seem to be better candidates for these tasks. And why kindling or drops of water or grains of sand? I feel certain that these items—as gifts for the devil—have their origins in European lore or maybe even in biblical sources, but I haven't been able to locate them.

The Cherokees gave turkey vultures the name *Suli* and felt that they played a role in shaping the earth at the time of creation, being responsible for the numerous mountains present in their homeland. This was because the great ancestral buzzard had agreed to fly over the earth and dry the mud with its flapping wings. But when he finally got to the Cherokee country, he was so tired that his flailing wings touched down, creating valleys. And as he lifted his wings, he created the mountains.

In the Cherokee myth called "The Daughter of the Sun: The Origins of Death" we are told that the northern cardinal is the metamorphosed form of the daughter of the sun. It's a complex story that I will summarize here from several sources.

The earth became dark after the sun's daughter was slain. The benevolent Little Men told the Cherokees they must go to *Tsusginai*, to "the Ghost country in *Usunhiyi*, the Darkening land in the west," and bring back the daughter in a box in order to restore light in their homeland.

The Little Men told them that they must take a box with them, and when they got to *Tsusginai* they would find all the ghosts at a dance. They must stand outside the circle, and when the young woman passed in the dance they must strike her with sourwood rods and she would fall to the ground. They must then put her into the box and bring her back to her mother. But they must be very sure not to open the box, even a little way, until they were home again.

This they did. On the way home, however, they heard the young woman wailing. She told them she had no air and was dying. They tried to withstand these pleas, but finally succumbed and lifted the lid of the box "just a little to give her air."

"There was a fluttering sound inside and something flew past them into the thicket and they heard a redbird cry, 'kwish! kwish! kwish!' in the bushes." They had lost the daughter of the sun.

Eventually the Cherokees did manage to appease the sun's grief with artful dancing and singing and the light returned. So

BLUE RIDGE NATURE JOURNAL

this is how we know that the redbird, which we call the cardinal, is the daughter of the sun.

Two of the more common birds the Cherokees observed year-round were the Carolina chickadee and the tufted titmouse. They named the chickadee *Tsikilili*, a word that imitates the bird's call. The titmouse they named *Utsugi*, which means "topknot" in reference to its crested head.

The chickadees and the titmice are closely related, are about the same size and act in somewhat the same fashion. In winter they forage together in loose, noisy flocks. It's usually the saucy, loud titmice that take the lead rather than the chickadees.

The Cherokees admired the more subdued personality of the chickadee, feeling the bird was an honest messenger that accurately foretold the coming of an absent friend or unknown stranger or even an enemy. The titmouse was considered to be a false messenger. For them, it was "the bird that lies."

These characteristics are embodied in the Cherokee myth about a terrible ogress named *Utlunta* or Spearfinger. This monster could assume any shape or appearance but usually appeared as an old woman, "excepting that her whole body was covered with a skin as hard as a rock that no weapon could wound or penetrate, and that on her right hand she had a long, stony forefinger of bone, like an awl or spearhead, with which she stabbed everyone to whom she get near enough." With her long finger she would extract the victim's liver—his essence— and eat it.

After many tries, the Indians finally trapped Spearfinger in a deep pitfall, "but shoot as true and as often as they could, their arrows struck the stony mail of the witch only to be broken and fall useless at her feet, while she taunted them and tried to climb out of the pit to get at them."

A titmouse came along and informed them in an arrogant manner that the only vulnerable part of the witch was her heart, but again their "arrows only glanced off with the flint heads broken." The Indians caught the titmouse and cut its tongue off, "so that ever since its tongue is short and everybody knows it is a liar."

Then a chickadee quietly appeared and alighted upon the witch's right hand as a signal of where her evil heart was actually located. An arrow directed there pierced the vital organ so that she fell dead. Ever since, for the Cherokees, the chickadee has been known as "the truth teller."

The Cherokee storytellers related these legends periodically for the entire village. The audience would include children and adults. For the adults, the story was about deception, reminding them that people and things aren't always as they appear. For the young people, the legend instructed them not to behave like the boastful lying titmouse, but like the truth-telling chickadee. That was the Cherokee way.

(Additional sources for this essay are Arlene Fradkin, *Cherokee Folk Zoology: The Animal World of a Native American People, 1700–1838*; Alan Kilpatrick, *The Night Has a Naked Soul: Witchcraft and Sorcery among the Western Cherokee*; and two volumes by James Mooney: *Myths of the Cherokees* and *The Swimmer Manuscript: Cherokee Sacred Formulas and Medical Prescriptions*.)

2.

WOLF LORE

THAT THE CUNNING OF THE WOLF EXCITED
THE ADMIRATION OF THE CHEROKEES THERE
CAN BE LITTLE DOUBT, AS DID HIS DISPLAY
OF COURAGE AND FEROCITY IN BATTLE,
AND HIS PROWESS AS A SUPERB LONG
DISTANCE HUNTER...NOR DID THE TRIBE
FAIL TO NOTICE THE ENVIABLE ADAPTATION
OF THE WOLF TO HIS ENVIRONMENT,
AS WELL AS HIS UNCANNY ABILITY TO
DETECT DANGER IN MINUTE CHANGES IN
TERRITORIAL DOMAIN. THEY ALSO SHARED
A REVERENCE FOR THE MOUNTAINS OF
THEIR HOMELAND.
—JANET AND DAVID C. CAMPBELL,
"THE WOLF CLAN" (1982)

In recent years otter, elk and other previously extirpated species have been successfully reintroduced in the Great Smoky Mountains National Park. A reintroduction of the red wolf in the Smokies was also attempted but then aborted. I can't, however, contemplate any scenario whereby timber wolves might be reintroduced anywhere in the Blue Ridge. Can you imagine the uproar if, say, the U.S. Fish and Wildlife Service asked for public input regarding a possible timber wolf release? That's not going to happen, but we can still remember the timber wolf and the time when it was the most menacing creature one could encounter in these hills.

The timber wolf, sometimes called the gray wolf, once ranged across most of North America, but no longer exists in the wild in the eastern United States. The most formidable of all the wild dogs of the world, it can measure over six feet in length, stand nearly a yard tall at the shoulder and weigh as much as 175 pounds.

In Cherokee lore he was revered as *Waya*—the companion of *Kanati*, their master hunter. One of his wolves had magic powers that enabled it to cure another wolf that had been bitten by a snake. Because of its ability to remain awake during the first seven days of creation, *Waya* was given the power of night vision so that it could be active at night and easily prey upon other animals for sustenance. Anthropologist James Mooney recorded in *Myths of the Cherokee* (1900) that,

> *in the beginning, the people say, the dog was put on the mountain and the wolf beside the fire. When winter came the dog could not stand the cold, so he came down to the settlement and drove the wolf from the fire. The wolf ran to the mountains, where it suited him so well that he prospered and increased, until after awhile he ventured down again and killed some animals in the settlements. The people got together and followed and killed him, but his brothers came from the mountain and took such revenge that ever since the people have been afraid to hunt the wolf.*

Mooney was told that an ordinary Cherokee would not kill a wolf "if he can possibly avoid it, but will let the animal go by unharmed, believing that the kindred of a slain wolf will surely revenge his death, and that the weapon with which the deed is done will be rendered worthless for further shooting until cleaned and exorcised by a medicine man." Designated killers, who followed elaborate rituals for atonement, could slay wolves that raided stock or fish traps.

The demise of the wolf in eastern North America began with the arrival of the colonial settlers, who brought an inbred fear and hatred of the "blood-thirsty varmint" from Europe. They were unwilling to tolerate raids on their livestock. The first wolf bounty in eastern North Carolina was set in 1748 at ten shillings for each wolf scalp, with other seaboard states adopting similar measures. Bounty hunters pursued their quarry with guns, dogs and wolf pits. After the American Revolution, the bounty climbed, in places, to as much as five dollars per scalp.

By the early 1800s, this intense pressure helped drive most of the remaining wolf population into the mountains, where skillful hunters familiar with the upcountry were required. The brothers Gideon and Nathan Lewis of Ashe County were among the first of the renowned wolf hunters in the Blue Ridge. According to John Preston Arthur's *Western North Carolina: A History (from 1730 to 1913)*, the brothers knew a good thing when they saw it. Upon locating a wolf den, one of the brothers would crawl in and secure the pups, from six to ten in each litter, as bounty. But somehow the mother wolf would always "escape." When asked why they never managed to kill a mature female, Gideon always replied matter-of-factly, "Would you expect a man to kill his milch-cow?"

In 1908, the schoolteacher Alexander S. Patton published a memoir titled *Memory Days*. Therein, he recollected wolf encounters that took place about 1850 in the Virginia portion of the Blue Ridge.

> *In that day wolves and bears made their homes in the dark caves and deep ravines of the mountains that lay, ridge after ridge, to the south of our homes. As children we often heard the night attack of bruin upon the pig-pen, and the raid upon the flock of sheep by ravenous wolves. In one night, a short time before this, the wolves had killed twenty sheep for my father. So we looked with dread upon these denizens of the forest, believing they would have no more regard for the feelings of a boy than for a sheep.*
>
> *One cloudy, sultry evening, when the atmosphere was in a suitable condition for the ready transmission of sound, we were returning from school, and as we were passing by the Hawk's Nest, all at once we heard a fierce howling and snarling apparently in the woods close to us. Aunt Rachel… cried, "Run children, the wolves are after us!"…On went*

the cavalcade, the children panting…the wolves still howling nearer and nearer! One of the boys struck his big toe against a rock and over he tumbled…holding his toe in one hand and screaming, "Oh, Lordy! The wolves will get me!"

"If you don't stop hollering the wolves will get you," cried Aunt Rachel. Taking the advice, he transferred all extra power to his heels, and forgetting his toe, he made up for lost time and soon caught up with the fleeing crowd. The woods seemed endless and the howls sounded louder! At last, almost breathless, we dashed out into the lane between two fields. "Stop children!" cried Aunt Rachel. "We are safe. The wolves are on the mountain."

That night those savage beasts kept up that dismal howling until twelve o'clock. There was no school the next day, but a grand wolf hunt was organized by the neighborhood. The hunt resulted in the killing of many and the driving of the others farther back from the settlements. As I think of that evening those howls still ring in my ears.

The period of the Civil War marked a resurgence of wolves when many excellent marksmen were pulled out of the mountains or otherwise occupied by the conflict. By the 1880s, however, the animals were again becoming scarce. According to William David Webster and the co-authors of *Mammals in the Carolinas, Virginia and Maryland* (1985) the "last gray wolf was killed in North Carolina in Haywood County in 1887 and in Virginia in 1910 in Tazewell County." But, in fact, wolf reports persisted in western North Carolina into the twentieth century.

Local records indicated that scalp bounties were paid in Swain and Clay Counties in North Carolina in 1889. One of the Swain County bounties, paid by the county commissioners, "allotted Q.L. Rose $5 for [a] wolf scalp." That was the legendary fiddle-player, storyteller, blockader, hunter and Civil War veteran Aquilla ("Quill") Rose. At the time, Rose was living on Eagle Creek in the Smokies. The most vivid portrait of him as a wolf hunter appeared in *The Heart of the Alleghanies or Western North Carolina* (1883) by Wilbur Zeigler and Ben Grosscup. The authors

visited Rose once to hunt deer. As they settled in to spend the night at his cabin, he obliged them with one of his tales:

"I was forced to cross a creek on some shelving rock above a waterfall. The rock was slick and I fell into a crevice, strikin' bottom on somethin' soft and hairy."

"A wolf?" someone asked.

"Yes, dog my skin!" Quill exclaimed. "Hit was the dry nest of a master old varmint under that fall. He was as fat as a bar jist shufflin' out o' winter quarters, an' he only had three legs. One gone at the knee. Chawed hit off, I reckon, to git shet of a trap. Well the wolf snarled and struggled like mad, but I had the holt on 'im. I didn't dare to lose my holt to git my knife, so I bent 'im down with my weight, and gittin' his head in the water drowned 'im in a few minutes. Then I toted and dragged 'im out to the dogs."

Zeigler and Grosscup subsequently verified that the story was true except for one notable point—in the telling, Quill had assumed the role of the actual hunter.

An editorial published in the early 1890s in the *Bryson City* (NC) *Times* mentioned wolves being "up around Clingmans Dome" in the Smokies. Unconfirmed sightings since 1900 in or near the national park, which was founded in 1934, were summarized in Donald W. Linzey's *Mammals of Great Smoky Mountains National Park* (1995). The most dramatic, as described in *The Asheville Citizen-Times*, took place near Tapoca, North Carolina. The newspaper related that in 1903 a "pack of 75 or 100 fierce wolves were denned in Hangover Mountain…just across the [Little] Tennessee River and often made raids upon sheep and cattle herds. Six years later the wolf pack was exterminated."

According to Linzey, "The most recent reported occurrence of the wolf in this area was related by the late G.S. Tennent of Asheville…A lone individual was killed by J.W. Parker, a patrolman for the Sherwood Forest Company near Waynesville, Haywood County, North Carolina, on February 27, 1933."

3.

PANTHER LORE

I frequently receive reports from readers of my natural history columns that they have encountered a panther at various sites in the Blue Ridge. I'd estimate that about 95 percent of these sightings are, in fact, of animals other than panthers. But the others—especially those made by farmers, experienced outdoorsmen and nature enthusiasts—seem to be fairly reliable.

For instance, I wrote a "Back Then" column about Cherokee panther lore for the March 8–14, 2006 issue of *Smoky Mountain News*. Of the ten or so e-mails I received from readers, only one seemed probable:

> *Dear George—I am a nature nut and…have participated in several of your seminars. I live in a community near Highlands, North Carolina. Five of us have seen panthers at different times during the last 3-5 years. We have compared notes regarding the description of the animal or animals we have seen and they are about identical. The cat I saw was at 1:15 p.m. on a bright sunny day. He jumped down off a small bank in front of my car while I was driving through the Kelsey Tract of the Nantahala National Forest. This cat was about 50-55 inches from nose to hips with about a 24-30 inch tail. It was rosy beige color fur except for a black goatee. Although I had a camera on the back seat of my car, before I could stop, the cat was almost out of sight. What a beautiful thing to behold!!! I was very excited the remainder of the week. Four other men here have seen what may be the same cat, all of them live within a half mile of the place of*

my sighting…About every two years we will hear the big cat scream during mating season. Anybody hearing that sound would agree that is the sound of A VERY BIG CAT. It gives you goose bumps all the way down your spine!!! We also notice that the rabbit population has taken a quantum drop during the period of these sightings. Possibly coyotes or foxes should get some credit for this. Just thought you would be interested. —Jim Whitehurst

I forwarded the correspondence to Bob Plott, a friend who lives in Statesville, North Carolina. Bob is a descendant of the mountain family that originally bred Plott hounds, perhaps the most renowned breed of hunting dog in North America. He is a founding member of Gist's Company of Scouts, a group named after Christopher Gist, the eighteenth-century North Carolina backwoodsman and scout. The group is made up of avid outdoorsmen who hunt and camp in extreme conditions, using only eighteenth-century weapons, clothing and gear. As such, they tend to be close and reliable observers of the natural world. Bob responded:

George—Thanks too, for the panther response from your reader. Charlie Brown and I have both seen big cats, fitting the description your reader gave, both in western North Carolina and in southwestern Virginia. In fact, a friend of mine who lives near Galax, Va., has a video of one in his backyard, going through garbage, and another friend saw one cross I-77 early one morning near Bland, Va. So there is no doubt in my mind that they are around, I am just surprised that someone hasn't hit one in a car, or a dead body of one has not been found somewhere. Of course, no hunter would ever leave evidence or admit that he or she had shot one, but I also know some boys who hunt down in S.C. who have seen them…The thing that I find odd, is that wildlife guys and rangers that I talk to, all vehemently deny the existence of the cougars in public, but privately acknowledge their existence, or at the very least issue their denials with a wink and a nod. So if everyone believes they are around, why all the denials? Just makes no sense to me. Take care, Bob.

Through the years, I've expressed the opinion that any panthers residing in the Blue Ridge today probably aren't descendants of the genetic stock that was originally here. My belief is that they are ones that have wandered into the Blue Ridge and adjacent region from Florida or the western states. Or, more likely, they are individuals trapped elsewhere (probably in the west) and deliberately released here. Whatever the truth, I'm reasonably certain that we do have panthers here, although I've never seen one.

Panthers—also called mountain lions, cougars and "painters"—are between 70 and 105 inches long, including the tail, which averages about 32 inches in length. Their body weight ranges between 100 and 220 pounds. They were fairly common into the very early twentieth century throughout remote portions of the Blue Ridge from Pennsylvania to Georgia. Donald W. Linzey noted in *Mammals of the Great Smoky Mountains National Park* (1995) that the last mountain lion killed in the Smokies was in the early winter of 1920.

In *Cherokee Folk Zoology: The Animal World of a Native American People, 1700–1838* (1990), Arlene Fradkin noted that the animal the Cherokees knew as *Tlvdaji* was given "the power to see and be active at night" after it displayed the "ability to remain awake the first seven nights of creation." Accordingly, it could easily "prey upon birds and mammals for sustenance."

In one of their sacred formulas, the Cherokees sang a song for the cure of frostbite titled "This, Whenever Their Feet Are Frost Bitten, Is The Cure." A translation in *The Swimmer Manuscript: Cherokee Sacred Formulas and Medicinal Prescriptions* (1932) by James Mooney and revised by Frans M. Olbrechts reads:

Thou art living, indeed. (Four times.)
There thou art living, indeed.
Thou art living, indeed. (Three times.)
Thou wizard, red Mountain Lion,
Thou art living, indeed.

This song was addressed to the panther because it supposedly had power over the ailment, its feet never being frostbitten. The word "red" indicated power. The actual treatment consisted of medicine men applying melted snow to the patient's frostbitten parts.

Deer were a panther's primary prey. In one of the Cherokee myths called "The Underground Panthers," a hunter and a panther collaborated in the killing of a buck. Anthropologist James Mooney collected this tale during the late 1880s and included it in his *Myths of the Cherokee* (1900). It is, in my opinion, one of the most hauntingly beautiful of the ancient Cherokee animal stories.

THE UNDERGROUND PANTHERS

A hunter was in the woods one day in winter when suddenly he saw a panther coming toward him and at once prepared to defend himself. The panther continued to approach, and the hunter was just about to shoot when the animal spoke. At once it seemed to the man as if there was no difference between them, and they were both of the same nature. The panther asked him where he was going, and the man said that he was looking for a deer.

"Well," said the panther, "we are getting ready for a Green-corn dance, and there are seven of us out after a buck, so we may as well hunt together."

The hunter agreed and they went on together. They started up one deer and another, but the panther made no sign, and said only, "Those are too small; we want something better." So the hunter did not shoot, and they went on.

They started up another deer, a larger one, and the panther sprang upon it and tore its throat, and finally killed it after a hard struggle. The hunter got out his knife to skin it, but the panther said the skin was too much torn to be used and they must try again.

They started up another large deer, and this one the panther killed without trouble, and then, wrapping his tail around it, threw it across his back. "Now, come to our townhouse," he said to the hunter.

The panther led the way, carrying the captured deer upon his back, up a little stream branch until they came to the headspring, when it seemed as if a door opened in the side of the hill and they went in. Now the hunter found himself in front of a large townhouse, with the finest *detsanun-li* [i.e., a level ground cleared for ceremonial purposes such as the Green Corn Ceremony] he had ever seen, and the trees around were green, and the air was warm, as in summer.

There was a great company there getting ready for the dance, and they were all panthers, but somehow it all seemed natural to the hunter. After a while the others who had been out came in with the deer they had taken, and the dance began. The hunter danced several rounds, and then said it was growing late and he must be getting home. So the panthers opened the door and he went out, and at once found himself alone in the woods again, and it was winter and very cold, with snow on the ground and on all the trees.

When he reached the settlement he found a party just starting out to search for him. They asked him where he had been for so long, and he told them the story, and then he found that he had been in the panther townhouse several days instead of only a very short time, as he had thought.

He died within seven days after his return, because he had already begun to take on the panther nature, and so could not live again with men. If he had stayed with the panthers he would have lived.

4.

BEAR LORE

Bears have always held a special attraction for humans. In a chapter titled "Killing the Sacred Bear" in *The Golden Bough: A Study in Magic and Religion* (1922), Sir James George Frazer traced the reverence for bears among the Ainu people of Japan and the Gilyats in Siberia. The Ainu thought of the bear as the *kamuni* (god) of the inanimate forces of nature and were themselves bear worshippers. Among the Gilyats, "the bear [was] the object of the most refined solicitude of an entire village and play[ed] the chief part in their religious ceremonies." Nevertheless, both the Ainu and the Gilyats killed and devoured bears with abandon.

Frazer concluded that the ancient hunter could "not afford to spare all animals" and was forced by necessity "to overcome his superstitious scruples and take the life of the beast. At the same time he does all he can to appease his victims and their kinfolk. Even in the act of killing them he testifies his respect for them, endeavors to excuse or even conceal his share in procuring their death, and promises that their remains will be honorably treated."

The ancient Cherokees knew the black bear as *Yona*. The designation *Yona Agisi* referred to a female bear, with *Yona Achvya* being a male bear. According to anthropologist James Mooney, the Cherokees also recognized a special "variety known as *Kalas-gunahita* (Long Hams)." This was an individual, Mooney surmised, "with long legs and small feet, which is always lean, and which the hunter does not care to shoot, possibly on account of its leanness." Cherokee acquaintances of mine believe that the *Kalas-gunahita* variety wasn't shot because the animal's lean torso, long legs and small feet made it look too much like a human being.

In *The Southeastern Indians* (1976), University of Georgia anthropologist Charles Hudson observed that, for the ancient Cherokees,

> *men and animals were not sharply separated, worlds apart, as they are in our thinking…But even though men and animals were interrelated, men were still set apart. Above all other animals, the bear represents the nature of the division between people and animals. According to a Cherokee oral tradition, bears are descended from a Cherokee clan who decided that they would prefer to live in the company of animals where they would never go hungry rather than face the toil and uncertainties of human existence.*

The clan that became bears told their human relatives: "When you yourselves are hungry come into the woods and call us and we shall come to give you our own flesh. You need not be afraid to kill us, for we shall live always."

As Arlene Fradkin pointed out in *Cherokee Folk Zoology* (1990), "The belief in the human origin of the bear was most probably based upon its ability to walk upright on two legs and the similarity of its tracks to human footprints." It might also be pointed out that to the non-trained eye the bones in a bear's forepaw so closely resemble the bones in human hands that the Federal Bureau of Investigation once issued a bulletin detailing the differences.

Accordingly, the Cherokees assigned human traits to the black bear and chronicled its quasi-human social activities in their myths. The great White Bear was the bear clan's chief. He lived at a place known as *Kuwahi* (Mulberry Place), which was located near a lake with medicinal powers in which wounded bears could bathe and recover. The townhouses of the bears were thought to be located under various high peaks in the Great Smoky Mountains. In these towns the bears assembled for councils and held dances, as did the Cherokees in their rituals.

Fradkin also noted that most bears were killed with abandon because the Cherokees had a firm belief in their powers of reincarnation. In one tale a bear "was resurrected to its proper form from the drops of its own spilt blood." In another, a bear "was allotted seven lives and was repeatedly killed by hunters until it finally died its last death."

Some day you might be hiking alone in the Smokies or some other remote area in the Blue Ridge. As you round a sharp bend in the trail on a high ridge, snuffling sounds come from the underbrush…the bushes part…a black form arises slowly on its hind legs and faces you, extending its front legs, like arms, in your direction. You will have encountered the wild spirit of the wilderness, *Yona*, the sacred animal that walks like a man.

5.

FOX LORE

In the natural world there are certain visual images that rivet the attention of human beholders. One of pure delight is a red fox suddenly glimpsed. Elizabeth and I have observed red foxes with some frequency through the years. But, for whatever reason, an encounter I had in the mid-1990s registered with me in particular detail. I was driving alone south of Asheville on the Blue Ridge Parkway. A light early morning mist was swirling in my truck's headlights. As if from out of nowhere, a fox suddenly appeared, moving across the roadway, nimble feet in a dainty trot. On the roadside embankment, it paused, lifted a front paw and turned to peer at the oncoming vehicle. The animal's eyes looked into mine without fear. It was simply curious. With heightened awareness, I could see drops of moisture clinging to the hairs that outlined the creature's silhouette. Then, with a single catlike bound, it disappeared in a graceful flow of movement. That clear image of a fox in the rain remains with me.

Sometimes a red fox will live up to its name in the sense that its fur is bright red. But most that we have seen were tawny rusty-red to reddish-yellow in coloration. Sometimes a red fox will resemble a gray fox. Since the latter often has some reddish tinges in its coat, the two species found in the Blue Ridge can be confused. But a gray fox is smaller than a red fox and the tip of its tail is dark gray or black. The red fox always has a white-tipped tail. Gray foxes prefer woodlands, often climb trees and are mostly nocturnal. Red foxes prefer more open areas, don't like to climb and are often about during daylight hours.

There has been some debate on whether the red fox is native to North America. In *The Audubon Society Field Guide to North American Mammals* (1980), John O. Whitaker Jr. noted that,

> *in the mid-eighteenth century, red foxes were imported from England and released in New York, New Jersey, Maryland, Delaware, and Virginia by landowners who enjoyed riding to the hounds. (At the time, the gray fox—not a good substitute for the red, as it cannot run as fast or as long—had not yet expanded its range north into these areas.) The red foxes that now populate almost all of the states are combined strains derived from the interbreeding of imported foxes with native races, which, encouraged by settlement, gradually expanded their range.*

In *The World of the Red Fox* (1969), Leonard Lee Rue III quoted New Englander Thomas Morton, who in 1634 recorded that "the Foxes are of two coloures; the one redd, the other gray…and are of good furre; they doe not stinke, as the Foxes of England."

Be that as it may, both the red fox (*Tsuhla*) and the gray fox (*Inali*) have secured places in Cherokee lore. If an individual setting off on a journey startled a fox that looked back and barked, this was a sure sign that a relative or neighbor would soon die. A fox howling near one's house warned of impending illness. But foxes could also be helpful. One of the Cherokees' sacred formulas contained an incantation evoking them as a cure for frostbite. Advance scouts sent out to locate enemies mimicked the barks and yips of foxes to stay in touch with one another. Portrayed in one of the stories as a quick-witted trickster, the fox was responsible for the loss of most of the bear's tail, which had at one time been long and bushy.

RACCOON LORE

Certain concepts about the natural world are so ingrained in our consciousness that we feel almost cheated when we find out they aren't true. Like many young people, I grew up reading books about animals. Among my favorites were the *Mother Westwind* stories, a series of books by Thornton W. Burgess. Raccoons frequently appeared in these books. One of them, as I recall, was even titled *The Adventures of Robby Raccoon*. Burgess's raccoons were invariably depicted as cute but mischievous critters who always washed their hands before eating. My mother made that trait into a model for behavior. Always washing one's hands before a meal became her moral equivalent of a raccoon's supposedly fastidious ways. It wasn't until many years later I discovered what raccoons are really up to when they take food to water.

Like opossums and coyotes, raccoons are well suited to the ever-changing lifestyles required in modern times. Their population numbers today are about the same as when the first settlers arrived. Their exceptionally agile hands allow raccoons to walk, swim, climb and open containers with ease, providing them with more food and shelter options than most animals.

When it comes to eating, they aren't picky. Frogs, fish, salamanders, shellfish, turtles, snakes, insects, worms, acorns, garbage and more are all fair game. Often they'll eat what they find without any further ado, but, if water is handy, they'll seek it out and dip the food into it with their forepaws. John O. Whitaker Jr. explained in *The Audubon Society Field Guide to North American Mammals* (1980) that "the objective…is not to clean the food, but rather to knead and tear at it, feeling for matter that should be rejected; wetting the paws enhances the sense of touch. In fact the common name comes from *aroughcoune*, used in colonial times by the Algonquin Indians of Virginia to mean 'he scratches with his hands.'"

Like the Algonquin, the Cherokees—who knew the raccoon as *Kvhli*—were close observers of the natural world. They paid special attention to the animal's clever ways and assigned to it a major role in their story of how the redbird (northern cardinal) became red.

HOW THE REDBIRD GOT HIS COLOR

A Raccoon passing a Wolf one day made several insulting remarks, until at last the Wolf became angry and turned and chased him. The Raccoon ran his best and managed to reach a tree by the river side before the Wolf came up. He climbed the tree and stretched out on a limb overhanging the water. When the Wolf arrived he saw the reflection in the water, and thinking it was the Raccoon he jumped at it and nearly drowned before he could scramble out again, all wet and dripping. He lay down on the bank to dry and fell asleep, and while he was sleeping the Raccoon came down the tree and plastered his eyes with dung. When the Wolf awoke he found he could not open his eyes, and began to whine. Along came a little brown bird through the bushes and heard the Wolf crying and asked what was the matter. The Wolf told the story and said, "If you will get my eyes open, I will show you where to find some nice red paint to paint yourself." "Alright" said the brown bird; so he pecked at the Wolf's eyes until he got off all the plaster. Then the Wolf took him to a rock that had streaks of bright red paint running through it, and the little bird painted himself with it, and has ever since been a Redbird.

—JAMES MOONEY, *MYTHS OF THE CHEROKEE* (1900)

7.

SKUNKS:

STRIPED AND SPOTTED

Hopefully, any encounter you have with a skunk will be a sighting, not a spraying. Neither Elizabeth nor I have ever been sprayed by a polecat. But our dogs have—and they were pitiful creatures for days afterward.

Five skunk species are resident in the United States: hooded skunks, hog-nosed skunks, western spotted skunks, eastern spotted skunks and striped skunks. Only the last two reside in the Blue Ridge. The striped skunk—which is black with two white stripes running up its back to form a cap on top of its head—is the one that usually comes to mind when someone starts telling skunk tales. In certain areas, however, the spotted skunk is the more common species. Sometimes referred to as a civet, the spotted skunk is black with a white spot on its forehead and under each ear. There are also four broken white stripes along its neck, back and sides, as well as a white-tipped tail.

The spotted skunk averages seventeen inches in length and three pounds in weight, while the larger striped skunk averages twenty-five inches and nine pounds. Both species den in rock outcrops, old woodchuck burrows and other readily available locations, including spaces in the foundations of human dwellings. In addition to eating fruit, they prey on a variety of insects, grubs and small mammals.

Now we get to the interesting part. The rear is, of course, the business end of a polecat. That's where you'll find the two vented anal glands that contain the potent, odoriferous fluid that can be sprayed with accuracy for distances of up to twelve or so feet. The mist from this fluid will often carry another thirty feet, while the nauseating odor will permeate the surrounding countryside for up to a mile. If need be, there is enough fluid in the anal glands to provide a skunk with up to six rounds of ammunition. Under normal circumstances, one blast is quite sufficient. Indeed, most predators are so wary once they spot a skunk's distinctive black-and-white markings that it can usually saunter through the woodlands without being disturbed.

When provoked, a striped skunk raises its plume-like tail daintily and assumes a U-shaped posture that allows its hip muscles to squeeze the fluid out of the anal glands. The spotted skunk has added embellishments, as described by Donald W. Linzey in *Mammals of Great Smoky Mountains National Park* (1995):

> *When frightened or angered, the eastern spotted skunk may engage in several unique behaviors that may serve as either a bluff or a warning prior to the discharge of the scent. It may stamp or pat its front feet in rapid succession on the floor or ground. It can also do a "handstand" on it front feet. The skunk upends itself, holds its tail in the air, and may walk up to several yards in this manner.*

In *Mammals of the Carolinas, Virginia and Maryland* (1985), David William Webster and the other authors of that volume observed that this handstand posture "allows the skunk to see where it aims its spray."

The ancient Cherokees knew both the striped and spotted skunk as *Dila*. Arlene Fradkin noted in *Cherokee Folk Zoology* (1990) that they believed its potent odor served as a counterbalance to contagious diseases. Scent glands were removed from carcasses, pierced with a small hole and hung over doorways. After the Civil War, one of the Cherokees who had served with the Union brought back smallpox to the Indian reservation from an infected camp near Knoxville. When he died a short time later, his funeral was widely attended by the Cherokees. The disease spread rampantly, quickly decimating the Cherokee population. Entire skunk bodies were hung up in the vain hope they would ward off the pestilence. Oil from the anal glands was rubbed directly upon infected people. Tribal members finally resorted to cooking and eating skunk meat.

Various odor-removal techniques are reported in the literature about skunks. But, if you do get sprayed, time is probably the only real cure. Wash out your eyes with water and burn or bury your clothes. Try not to think about what happened. Don't go out in public for a while.

8.

MOUNTAIN BOOMERS:

"OUR SPEEDIEST VARMINT"

It seems to me that the general reputation of squirrels has declined within my lifetime. I don't recall hearing negative remarks about squirrels when I was growing up. Most folks I encountered back then seemed to hold them in rather high esteem. That's no longer the case. It's my guess that this turnabout took place because of the explosion in bird watching and feeding that has occurred in the last thirty or so years. Because squirrels are so adroit and persistent at raiding bird feeders, they are now quite often referred to as "tree rats."

But I like squirrels and will continue to defend their antics whenever possible. After all, they're just doing what squirrels are programmed to do, which is to rather obsessively gather and store food in great quantities. Without gray squirrels we wouldn't have the widespread oak forests that are one of the crowning glories of eastern North America. And you have to admit that watching a squirrel execute a well-planned raid on a bird feeder can be as interesting as watching a well-executed double play in baseball. It's all about grace, balance and timing.

There are five species of tree squirrel resident in the Blue Ridge: gray squirrels, fox squirrels, red squirrels, northern flying squirrels and southern flying squirrels. My favorite is the red squirrel, which is often known locally as the "mountain boomer." I have also heard them called "pine" squirrels because, unlike gray squirrels, which prefer oak forests and acorns, these little creatures often frequent conifer stands to feed upon seeds. In the Blue Ridge, they are found primarily in hemlock and spruce-fir forests, but sometimes they'll frequent mixed conifer-hardwood forests.

A gray squirrel will average about eighteen inches in length and sometimes weigh a pound, while a boomer will be about twelve inches and hardly exceed half a pound. Its reddish-dark back and light belly are separated in summer by a lateral black stripe. The tail hairs are yellow tipped.

There is a prominent white ring around each eye that gives the little animal a constantly alert appearance. I am of the opinion that these eye rings act as light collectors, allowing boomers to see better in dim light conditions than would otherwise be the case. Some deep forest bird species—such as the blue-headed vireo, for example—have similar markings for that reason.

In addition to seeds, boomers will eat acorns, beechnuts, walnuts and similar fare. Researchers who have investigated their nests often find parts of mushrooms that have been carefully cut and carried into a tree cavity. There they are wedged into a crevice to dry before being eaten. Based on this evidence, it appears that boomers readily devour *Amanita* and other poisonous mushrooms that would kill a human.

Boomers are so pugnacious and feisty that a "tree warrior" legend has evolved; indeed, red squirrels are so highly successful in their battles with gray squirrels that some hunters I have encountered in western North Carolina have accused them of castrating their rivals. Gray squirrels lacking testes are cited as evidence. Actually, adult male gray squirrels retract their testes into the body wall so that they are not seen except during the breeding season.

Boomers are so quick that legends regarding their speedy movements also have persisted. In 1986, western North Carolina folklorist and *Asheville Citizen-Times* newspaper columnist John Parris devoted a three-part series to boomers. The first installment was titled "The 'Boomer' Is Our Speediest Varmint." It opened with this paragraph:

There's no animal as fast as the mountain boomer, the little red squirrel that haunts our high-altitude forests. "He's so fast," said Lindsey Rogers, a mountain man who grew up at a time when the woods were full of boomers, "he can cut a buckeye off the limb of a tree and outrun it to the ground. He'll be standing there and looking up by the time it hits the ground."

9.

HONEYBEE LORE

Honey was a primary sweetening agent for the early settlers throughout the Blue Ridge. And to this day, of course, numerous beekeepers in the region trace the origins of their activity to the introduction of the honeybee into North America. Prior to that time, sweetening was obtained primarily by tapping maple trees.

The honeybee probably arrived on this continent during the 1600s. They became so numerous that American Indians called them the "white man's fly." Donald Edward Davis noted in *Where There Are Mountains: An Environmental History of the Southern Appalachians* (2000) that

> *by the time of the American Revolution…William Bartram found honeybees numerous "from Nova Scotia to East Florida." During his tour of the Cherokee country in 1796, Benjamin Hawkins reported that the Cherokees already "had bees and honey" and were doing "a considerable trade in beeswax." Moreover, European plants such as apple trees were greatly dependent on the pollination of honeybees in order to consistently bear fruit. Certainly the honeybee also helped native plants, including Indian maize, to produce more prolifically.*

As previously noted, sourwood trees produced the region's most famous honey and black gum trees, which are usually hollow, were used to make bee gums. The white settlers simply sectioned a black gum, placed it on end with boards on the top and bottom, and made an entrance hole. Gums were also constructed from rough planks.

Obtaining a hive of bees was the next step. Some bee hunters located a watering place for bees and followed them back to their homes in hollow trees. Others baited the bees with corn cobs soaked in honey and then followed them home. If their home base couldn't be easily located, the hunter simply kept setting out more bait until he finally found it.

In *Foxfire 2* (1973), a volume compiled and edited by Elliott Wigginton and his students in north Georgia, the recipe for a unique "stink-bait" bee attraction recipe is provided. One veteran bee hunter recalled that it was virtually foolproof: "Old-timers used to put corn cobs and dirt in a bucket, urinate in it, and then leave it for a few days. When they got back, the bees would be there."

The same bee hunter told Wigginton's students that he "would set up two bait locations, one a short distance from the other. When the lines from each were established, one had simply to follow each to the point where they intersected, and there would be the tree. When the tree was located, a deep X or other sign was almost always cut into the bark. Such a mark was understood by the whole community as meaning that that particular tree was already someone's property and thus could not be cut or interfered with."

A bee tree could be felled in any season, but the best time was in September when the bee hunter could rob both honey and bees. He would bring an ax (to fell the tree), a tub (for the honey) and bee gum or tow sack (for the bees). Once the tree was down, he'd locate the queen and place her in front of the gum or tow sack. In short order, both she and her attendants would crawl into the enclosures and be relocated at a site near the bee hunter's cabin.

Through the years a considerable amount of lore has become associated with the varied aspects of beekeeping. In *Mountain Bred* (1967), for instance, John Parris devoted a chapter titled "When the Master Dies Move the Bees" to a conversation he'd had with Paul Gibson, then a county farm agent in western North Carolina.

"There's a lot of superstitions about bee-keeping," Paul said. "One is, if a colony of bees swarm you've got to get out and ring a bell or beat on a dishpan before they'll settle. I don't know why folks believe in it, for bees don't have a hearing organ. They go by physical vibrations.

"Then there's the one old-timers swear by. They say if the master dies the bees die with him, unless the bees are moved."

To check out this latter belief, Parris sought out Eliza Jane Bradley, age eighty-seven, who was at that time the recent widow of a master beekeeper.

"Yes, the bees are all right," she said. "We moved 'em before we took the Old Man out of the house. I saw to that no sooner than I saw he was dead. You know, they always say that if you don't move the bees when the master dies you'll lose them. They'll die, too. We just moved 'em about an inch…Just so they wasn't like he had put 'em. Ever'body'll tell you it don't matter how much you move 'em, just so as you move 'em.

"Well, the Old Man died about 3:30 in the morning. Right away we sent to Bryson City for the undertaker. And the very next thing, I told one of my boys that the bees would have to be moved. He and another fellow went out—it was still dark and cold—and moved the bees. There was 23 stands. Since then I've lost but two….Now, I know, as sure as I'm a-settin' here, if them bees hadn't of been moved there wouldn't be a one out there now. I know what I'm talkin' about."

10.

CHEROKEE COOKERY:

YELLOW JACKET SOUP

AND MORE

During the late 1880s, anthropologist James Mooney spent parts of three years in the Big Cove community of the Qualla Boundary (present Cherokee, North Carolina) recording the history and lifestyles of the remnant Eastern Band of Cherokee Indians. In regard to food, he observed in *Myths of the Cherokee* (1900) that "the Indian is a thorough believer in the doctrine that 'man is what he eats.' A continuous adherence to the diet commonly used by a bear will finally give to the eater the bear's nature, if not also the bear form. A certain term of 'white man's food' will give the Indian the white man's nature, so that neither the remedies nor the spells of the Indian doctor will have any effect upon him." In other words, food was important to the Cherokees not only for sustenance but also as a spiritual regimen.

In *The Southeastern Indians* (1976), University of Georgia anthropologist Charles Hudson noted that "the Southeastern Indians did not eat regular meals. They ate whenever they were hungry…They ate food from pottery or gourd containers or from shallow wooden bowls carved out of gum, poplar, box elder, sycamore, or elm. They ate with large spoons made from gourds, wood, or bison horn, and they also ate with their fingers."

In regard to what many might consider to be the more exotic foods in their diets, Hudson also observed that, "when faced with the prospect of starvation, the Southeastern Indians knew techniques for eating snakes, lizards, frogs, snails, and insects. Indeed into the present century some Cherokee women knew a recipe for making a soup out of yellow jacket larvae and a recipe for fried locusts."

I had wondered how yellow jacket soup was prepared since encountering the mention of it in Hudson's book. So, I was pleased a year or so ago to happen upon a recipe posted on the Internet under the heading, "The Chief Cooks: Traditional Cherokee Recipes By Principal Chief Wilma Mankiller" (1988). Wilma Mankiller was the former principal chief of the Cherokee Nation of Oklahoma. I had had the good fortune to observe her at the first official reunion of the Eastern and Western Cherokees, which took place at Red Clay, Tennessee, in 1984. She was then the vice-chief, but even at that point in her career she was a very forceful and articulate individual. It didn't occur to me then to introduce myself and ask if she might have a recipe for yellow jacket soup. Here it is:

Yellow Jacket Soup
Ingredients: Ground-dwelling yellow jackets
Directions: Although the mention of "yellow jacket soup" immediately raises an eyebrow on those unaccustomed to such a food, it is actually a delicacy and should not be criticized until tried. Only the bravest should dare to try this dish!! Secure an entire nest of ground-dwelling yellow jackets when it is full of grubs. Loosen all the uncovered grubs by heating and removing them. Heat the nest with the remaining grubs over a fire until the thin, paper-like covering parches. Pick out the yellow jackets and brown them over the fire. Cook the browned yellow jackets in boiling water to make soup and season to taste.
Note: Yellow jackets are easily angered and swarm. Obtaining a nest of these insects should only be done…by people who are experienced in collecting insects.

Yellow jacket soup wasn't the only exotic dish relished by the Cherokees. Here are some recipes excerpted from *Cherokee*

Cooklore: Preparing Cherokee Foods (1951), a pamphlet compiled by Samuel E. Beck and Mary Ulmer Chiltoskey.

Toads—*Catch toads, twist off their heads, pull off the skin while all the time holding the animal under running water lest the meat become very bitter. Parboil, then cook as any other meat.*

Knee-deeps—*Catch early frogs, called knee-deeps, scald and skin. Parboil and cook like other meats.*

Blood pudding—*When butchering an animal, have a bucket handy with salt in the bottom to catch the blood as soon as the animal is stuck. Stir the blood to keep it from clotting. When the pouch is removed, clean it well, add a little fat to the blood as it is put into the pouch and add black pepper. Sew up the opening of the pouch, put into a pot of water and boil until done. Set aside to cool before slicing to serve.*

Crayfish—*Catch crayfish by baiting them with groundhog meat or buttermilk. Pinch off the tails and legs to use. Parboil, remove the hulls and fry the little meat that is left. When crisp it is ready to eat. May also be made into soup or stew after being fried.*

Locust—*Gather the locusts (cicadas) at night immediately after they have left their shells, wash and fry them in a small amount of grease. Eat these hot or cold. Be sure that you gather the locusts before the sun hits them or they will not be good. If you gather them before they split out of their shells, they only have to be peeled to be ready to wash and fry.*

11.

TLANUWAS AND *UKTENAS*

THE CHEROKEES BELIEVED THAT THEY MUST KEEP THE WORLD IN BALANCE, IN A STATE OF EQUILIBRIUM...THAT IF THEY DID NOT MAINTAIN EQUILIBRIUM, THEN DROUGHTS, STORMS, DISEASE, OR OTHER DISASTERS MIGHT OCCUR...THEY TRIED NOT TO EXPLOIT NATURE. WHEN A HUNTER KILLED A DEER, FOR EXAMPLE, HE PERFORMED A SPECIAL RITUAL IN WHICH HE APOLOGIZED TO THE SPIRIT OF THE DEER AND EXPLAINED THAT HIS FAMILY NEEDED FOOD. HUNTERS NEVER KILLED FOR SPORT. THEY BELIEVED THAT IF THEY VIOLATED THEIR SACRED TRUST, TERRIBLE THINGS WOULD HAPPEN TO THEM. THE EXPLOITATION OF ANIMALS COULD BRING DISEASE. IF THIS HAPPENED, PLANTS, WHICH WERE A NATURAL COUNTERBALANCE TO ANIMALS, COULD PROVIDE A CURE.
—THEDA PERDUE, *THE CHEROKEE* (1989)

On one level, the natural history of a region consists of its terrain, habitats, plants, animals and how they interrelate. Elizabeth and I also believe that no full understanding of the natural history of a region can be realized without coming to terms with its spiritual landscape. And when we consider the spiritual landscape of the Blue Ridge, we enter the realm of the ancient Cherokees.

They called themselves the *Ani-Yun-wiya*, which signified they were the Principal People. As such, the Cherokees assumed that it was their responsibility to maintain harmony and balance—not only in their homeland but also in the universe. They did so by invoking the powers of the Upper World to help them neutralize the powers of the Under World, in order to bring balance and peace into the mundane Middle World occupied by humans and the four-legged animals.

Quite naturally, birds epitomized the Upper World—the realm of light and everlasting life. The Cherokees were keen observers of bird life here in the Blue Ridge. As we do today, they admired birds for their beauty, for their ability to sing and—most of all—for their ability to fly.

As part of their belief system, they envisioned a mythic bird—probably modeled on the peregrine falcon—known as the *Tlanuwa* or Mythic Hawk. This was a large and ferocious bird noted for its swift and strong flight. Numerous cliffs throughout the Cherokee country were designated as places where *Tlanuwas* resided. These, no doubt, were also places where peregrine falcons nested in ancient times.

The Cherokees held the *Tlanuwas* in high esteem because they were the mortal enemies of the *Uktenas*, the giant serpents that represented the Under World—the realm of darkness and everlasting death. While living with the Eastern Band of Cherokee Indians in western North Carolina during the late 1880s, anthropologist James Mooney collected *Uktena* lore subsequently published as part of *Myths of the Cherokee* (1900). To this day, a conversation about *Uktenas* can be conducted with many of the more traditional Cherokees—who sometimes refer to it as "the *Ukten*"—so that, in a metaphorical sense, the creature lives on.

A snake myth requires a big serpent, and the legend of the *Uktena* was no exception. According to Mooney's informants, the creature—which had been born of envy and anger—was "as large around as a tree trunk, with horns on its head, and a bright blazing crest like a diamond upon its forehead, and scales glittering like sparks of fire. It has rings or spots of color along its whole length and cannot be wounded except by shooting in the seventh spot from the head, because under this spot are its heart and life." *Uktenas* were often described as having large sets of antlers. The most compelling physical feature, however, was a diamond-shaped crest (often depicted as a quartz crystal) on its forehead that emitted flashes of light like a blazing star. Those encountering the serpent—especially young children—were so bedazzled by this light that they were lured, like a moth to a flame, toward certain death.

But in the ancient Cherokee spirituality system there was always a balance between good and evil. Their medicine men utilized various crystals to foresee the future and restore balance. The most powerful crystal of all was the *ulunsuti*—the jewel embedded in an *Uktena*'s head. Such a stone, they felt, ensured "success in hunting, love, rainmaking, and other undertakings, but the greatest use is in divination, so that when it is evoked for this purpose by its owner the future is mirrored in the transparent crystal as a tree is reflected in the quiet stream below."

For the most part, *Uktenas* lived on the margins of the Cherokee world—like dark shadows in a dream—in the deep pools of rivers or lonely passes in the high mountains. From generation to generation, these sites were carefully designated as "where the *Uktena* stays" to warn the unwary not to venture near them. But if a Cherokee warrior was brave enough to venture into the dreaded place where an *Uktena* resided, he could evoke the spirit of the Upper World in the guise of the *Tlanuwa* to accompany him. Together, they would be able to slay the serpent, extract the *ulunsuti* from its forehead and bring it home to the *Ani-Yun-wiya* to restore peace and harmony in the mundane world. It's a fable about the eternal battle between order and chaos.

(Additional sources for this topic are James Adair, *The History of the American Indians*; Arlene Fradkin, *Cherokee Folk Zoology: The Animal World of a Native American People, 1700–1838*; and two publications by Charles Hudson: *The Southeastern Indians* and "Uktena: A Cherokee Anomalous Monster," which appeared in the *Journal of Cherokee Studies*.)

12.

COPPERHEADS AND TIMBER RATTLERS

Snakes are among the world's most beautiful creatures. There are twenty-three species in the Blue Ridge, some being common throughout and others infrequent to rare. In my experience, the most commonly encountered species include black racers, rat snakes, ringneck snakes, rough green snakes, queen snakes, eastern garter snakes, northern water snakes and northern copperheads. There are two poisonous snakes: northern copperheads and timber rattlesnakes. Both use heat-sensitive organs in their facial pits to detect prey.

Because of the natural history columns I write, readers frequently contact me to report what they assume are encounters with cottonmouth moccasins. But those aquatic and sluggish serpents are generally scarce outside the coastal plain and, to my knowledge, have never been reported in the Blue Ridge. I suspect those making these reports are, in fact, encountering northern water snakes—a species that is often hyperactive and aggressive in and around water, but isn't poisonous.

The northern copperhead is by far the most commonly encountered of our poisonous snakes, being found in a variety of habitats from the lowest elevations to more than 4,000 feet—but usually not above 2,500 feet. They often hide in rock walls or beneath boards and pieces of tin near rural homes. Since they're adept at burrowing into sawdust piles, most sawmills have resident copperheads. They are stout-bodied, averaging about twenty-four to thirty inches in length. Individuals more than four feet in length are rare. Immature copperheads have bright greenish-yellow tails. Adults display brown or chestnut hourglass-shaped cross-bands over a brown, tan or pinkish body color. The top of the head has large, symmetrical coppery-red to yellowish-brown plates. Under most circumstances, this natural camouflage makes the serpent virtually invisible.

"I've pointed out copperheads in the woods to people who couldn't see them at all until I picked the snake up and showed it to them," said Charles Willis, an acquaintance of mine who used to catch copperheads and rattlesnakes with his hands as a hobby. "It's a puzzle folks don't get bit more often. I guess they just step right over them and keep on going. I've even found copperheads in parking lots here in Bryson City. They're just about everywhere."

Apparently that's true. Some years ago, William Hardy, the longtime director of the popular *Unto These Hills* outdoor drama in Cherokee, North Carolina, told me about an evening when "a nest of copperheads" was discovered at one end of the outdoor stage. The remainder of that evening's production was performed at the other end of the stage.

Reports of copperheads coming into homes are not unusual. *Asheville Citizen-Times* columnist Bob Terrell was told by Michael Medlin that while his sister was being married at his home on Wolf Creek in Graham County, North Carolina, a copperhead showed up. "Happened in my living room," Medlin recalled. "Right in the middle of the shebang, out from under the couch crawled this big copperhead. The room cleared like somebody had thrown a live grenade in the window."

Timber rattlesnakes are not nearly as common in settled areas as copperheads. They're found from the lowest elevations up to six-thousand feet, but are rare in the high-elevation spruce-fir forests. Like copperheads, they generally prefer rocky habitats. In summer, however, rattlesnakes seek prey throughout the forests, meadows and farmlands of the Blue Ridge, frequently "holing up" in old stumps. Stephen G. Tilley and James E. Huheey noted in *Reptiles & Amphibians of the Smokies* (2001) that "timber

rattlesnakes overwinter, often with copperheads and other snakes, in deep crevices on rocky, usually south-facing slopes. Some of these dens have probably been utilized for centuries or millennia."

Rattlesnakes are heavy-bodied, averaging thirty-six to fifty-four inches in length. A five-foot specimen is unusual, but they can be more than six feet in length. There are two color phases: a yellow phase with wavy cross-bands down the back over a body color of yellow, brown or gray; and a black phase in which individuals are very dark or entirely black.

The most distinctive feature of the rattlesnake is, of course, its rattle. Poisonous snakes prefer not to waste energy or venom except in pursuing food. The rattle serves to warn off creatures that might disturb or harm the serpent. Some authorities think the evolution of the rattle occurred by natural selection years ago when the rattlesnake's ancestors were in danger of being trampled by vast herds of grazing animals. Whatever its origin, the rattle is an effective instrument. It's a sound that galvanizes the senses. The tail vibrates with an uncanny almost-musical warning—you freeze in mid-step, holding your breath but unaware that you're doing so…the hair on the back of your neck stands on end…the moment remains imprinted in your memory bank.

This rattle consists of a series of loosely interlocking segments composed of keratin, the same material that is in animal horns and human fingernails. Through transverse vibrations of the tail, these segments produce a sound that has been most frequently described as a "buzzing," but it has also correctly been likened to escaping steam or the sound produced by cicadas. The good news is that, if the rattlesnake is large, the warning can be heard for several hundred feet. The bad news is that rattlesnakes don't always sound a warning before striking. If you don't heed the warning or if it comes too late or not at all, the chunky arrowhead-shaped head cocked above the coiled muscular body will deliver its venom load in a strike quicker than an eye-blink.

The bites of both copperheads and rattlesnakes are reported to be extremely painful. But the toxic agents in rattlesnake venom are far more powerful and more likely to result in a human fatality if not attended to professionally. Dr. Harold Bacon, who practiced medicine in Bryson City from 1935 until his death in the early 1990s, treated a large number of snakebites during his career. He told me the most severe had occurred before the days of indoor plumbing. During hot midsummer afternoons, mountain women would go to their spring, kneel down to draw water and sometimes be bitten in the neck by a poisonous snake attracted to the cool setting. Whenever I asked him what someone should do when bitten by a poisonous snake, Dr. Bacon would always remove his car keys from his pocket and hold them up. That was his way of saying not to fool around in the woods with primitive remedies but to get to a car and drive to a hospital.

IV. Paintings

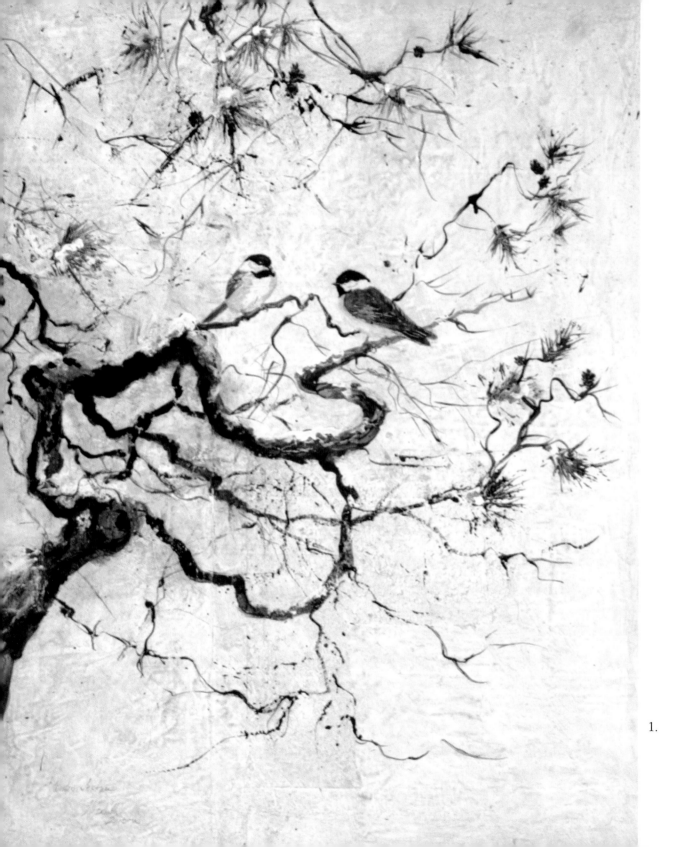

1.

2.

3.

4.

5.

6.

7.

8.

9.

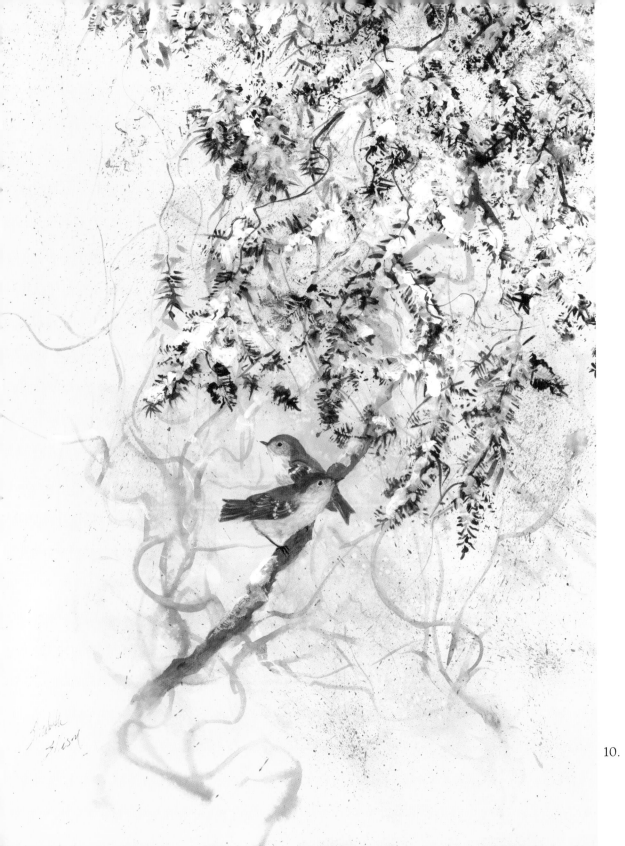

10.

11.

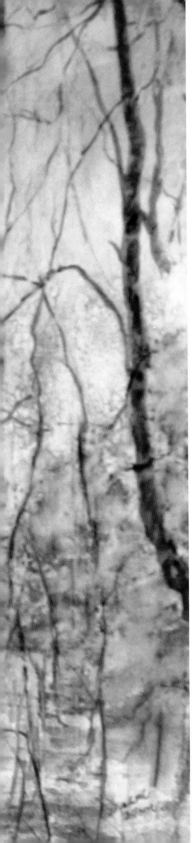

12.

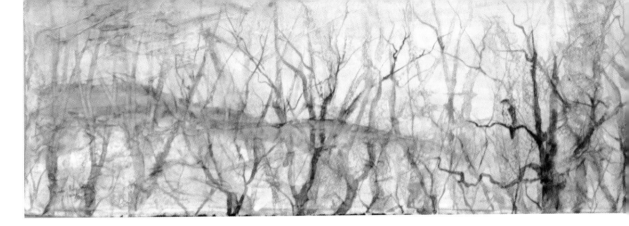

13.

14.

15.

16.

17.

18.

19.

20.

21.

22.

23.

24.

25.

26.

27.

"Morning Light"
Elizabeth
Ellison

28.

29.

30.

31.

32.

33.

35.

34.

36.

37.

38.

39.

ARTWORK SPECIFICATIONS

1. *Winter Texture*, mixed media, 23 x 30 inches
2. *Another Cold Day in the Mountains*, watercolor 30 x 22 inches
3. *Fall Color at Big Rock*, watercolor, 41 x 25, inches
4. *Along the Tuckasegee River*, watercolor, 24 x 18 inches
5. *Below the Falls: Indian Creek*, mixed media, 22 x 30 inches
6. *Light in the Mountains*, watercolor, 40 x 13 inches
7. *Old McHan Hotel: Whittier, NC*, watercolor, 30 x 22 inches
8. *Winged Spirit*, mixed media on handmade yucca paper, 38 x 22 inches
9. *Traveling Companions: Barn Swallows*, mixed media, 40 x 25 inches
10. *Ruby-Crowned Kinglets*, mixed media, 18 x 24 inches
11. *White-Throated Sparrows*, watercolor, 24 x 18 inches
12. *The Slough at Ferguson Fields*, mixed media, 24 x 18 inches
13. *The Ridge in Winter*, mixed media, 30 x 11 inches
14. *Our Spirits Sang with the Falling Water*, mixed media, 18 x 24 inches
15. *Nellie's Barn*, mixed media, 22 x 30 inches
16. *Winter Light: Studio View*, watercolor, 40 x 13 inches
17 and 18. *There is a Story Here*, diptych, watercolor, 30 x 22 inches
19. *The Master Gardener*, watercolor, 24 x 18 inches
20. *Roadside Decoration: Joe Pye Weed*, watercolor, 18 x 24 inches
21. *Into Cataloochee Valley*, watercolor, 18 x 24 inches
22. *In Perfect Harmony*, watercolor, 24 x 18 inches

23. *Southern Grandeur*, watercolor, 30 x 22 inches
24. *Trail Walking*, watercolor, 41 x 25 inches
25. *The Ridge in Summer*, watercolor, 30 x 12 inches
26. *A Play of Light*, watercolor, 30 x 22 inches
27. *Mist Rhythm*, watercolor, 30 x 22 inches
28. *Morning Light*, watercolor, 30 x 22 inches
29. *Wetland Inhabitants: Irises and Common Yellowthroat*, watercolor, 22 x 30 inches
30. *Daisy Fields*, watercolor, 24 x 18 inches
31. *Nantahala Gorge*, watercolor, 30 x 22 inches
32. *An Ancient Trail*, mixed media, 23 x 30 inches
33. *Oconaluftee at Kephart Prong*, watercolor
34. *Rainbow Springs*, watercolor, 41 x 25 inches
35. *Waterrock Knob in Winter*, mixed media, 30 x 22 inches
36. *And Then the Ridges*, watercolor, 41 x 25 inches
37. *Autumn Glory*, watercolor, 41 x 25 inches
38. *The Tuckasegee in Fall*, watercolor, 30 x 22 inches
39. *A July Sunset: Lake Fontana*, watercolor, 40 x 13 inches

SOURCES

Anon. 1898. "Bird Superstitions and Winged Portents." *Birds*, May.
———. 1971. "Service." *The Compact Edition of the Oxford English Dictionary*. NY: Oxford University Press.
———. 1994. *Joyce Kilmer-Slickrock Wilderness and Citico Creek Wilderness in the Nantahala and Cherokee National Forests*. Atlanta: United States Department of Agriculture, Forest Service, Southern Region.
———. n.d. *Cove Hardwood Self-guiding Nature Trail*. Gatlinburg, TN: Great Smoky Mountains Association in cooperation with the National Park Service.
———. n.d. *Revitalization of Traditional Cherokee Artisan Resources*. http://www.rtcar.org/#.
Adair, James. 1775. *The History of the American Indians*. London: Printed for Edward and Charles Dilly, in the Poultry.
Amoroso, J. 2002. "Wild Ideas: The Odor of Galax." *Chinquapin: The Newsletter of the Southern Appalachian Botanical Society* 10 (Summer).
Arthur, John Preston. 1914. *Western North Carolina: A History (from 1730 to 1913)*. Asheville, NC: Edward Buncombe Chapter of the Daughters of the American Revolution.
Atwood, Wallace W. 1940. *The Physiographic Provinces of North America*. Boston: Ginn and Company.
Beck, Samuel E., and Mary Ulmer Chiltoskey. 1951. *Cherokee Cooklore: Preparing Cherokee Foods*. Cherokee, NC: Published by Mary and Goingback Chiltoskey.
Bernhardt, Peter. 1989. *Wily Orchids & Underground Orchids: Revelations of a Botanist*. NY: William Morrow and Company.
Bierzychudek, Paulette. 1982. "Jack and Jill in the Pulpit." *Natural History Magazine* 91 (March).
Bir, Richard. 1992. *Growing and Propagating Showy Native Woody Plants*. Chapel Hill: University of North Carolina Press.
Brooks, Maurice. 1965. *The Appalachians*. Boston: Houghton Mifflin Co.
Brown, Claud A., and L. Katherine Kirkman. 1990. *Trees of Georgia and Adjacent States*. Portland, OR: Timber Press.
Brown, Fred, and Nell Jones. 1998. *Highroad Guide to the Georgia Mountains*. Atlanta: Longstreet.

Byer, Fred. 1991. *North Carolina: The Years Before Man: A Geologic History*. Durham, NC: Carolina Academic Press.
Campbell, Janet, and David G. Campbell. 1982. "The Wolf Clan." *Journal of Cherokee Studies* 7 (Fall).
Caras, Roger A. 1967. *North American Mammals: Fur-Bearing Animals of the United States and Canada*. New York: Galahad.
Carter, Mark W., Carl E. Merschat, and William F. Wilson. 1999. *A Geologic Adventure Along the Blue Ridge Parkway in North Carolina*. Raleigh: Bulletin 98, NC Geologic Survey Section.
Conners, John A. 1988. *Shenandoah National Park: An Interpretive Guide*. Blacksburg, VA: McDonald & Woodward Publishing Company.
Constantz, George. 1994. *Hollows, Peepers, and Highlanders: An Appalachian Mountain Ecology*. Missoula, MT: Mountain Press Publishing Co.
Davis, Donald Edward. 2000. *Where There Are Mountains: An Environmental History of the Southern Appalachians*. Athens: University of Georgia Press.
Elliott, Douglas B. 1976. *Roots: An Underground Botany and Forager's Guide— The Useful Wild Roots, Tubers, Corms and Rhizomes of North America*. Old Greenwich, CT: The Chatham Press.
Ellison, George. 2005. *Mountain Passages: Natural and Cultural History of Western North Carolina and the Great Smoky Mountains*. Charleston, SC: The History Press.
Evans, Murray. 2005. *Ferns & Fern Allies of the Smokies*. Gatlinburg, TN: Great Smoky Mountains Association.
Ewan, Joesph, and Nesta Ewan. 1963. "John Lyon, Nurseryman and Plant Hunter, and His Journal, 1799–1814." *Transactions of the American Philosophical Society* 53 (pt. 2).
Faulkner, Herbert Waldron. 1917. *The Mysteries of the Flowers*. NY: Frederick A. Stokes Company.
Fenneman, Nevin M. 1938. *Physiography of [the] Eastern United States*. NY: McGraw-Hill Book Company, Inc.
Fradkin, Arlene. 1990. *Cherokee Folk Zoology: The Animal World of a Native American People, 1700–1838*. New York: Garland.
Frazer, James George. 1922. *The Golden Bough: A Study in Magic and Religion*. NY: The Macmillan Co.
Gilfillan, Merrill. 1997. *Burnt House to Paw Paw: Appalachian Notes*. West Stockbridge, MA: Hard Press, Inc.
Godfrey, Michael. 1975. *A Closer Look*. San Francisco: Sierra Club Books.
Gould, Stephen Jay. 1985. *The Flamingo's Smile*. NY: W.W. Norton Co.
Guerrant, Edward. 1910. *The Galax Gatherers: The Gospel Among the Highlanders*. Richmond, VA: Onward Press.
Hallowell, Anne C., and Barbara G. Hallowell. 2001 (rev. ed.). *Fern Finder: A Guide to Native Ferns of Central and Northeastern United States and Eastern Canada*. Rochester, NY: Nature Study Guild Publishers.
Hamel, Paul B., and Mary U. Chiltoskey. 1975. *Cherokee Plants and Their Uses—A 400 Year History*. Sylva, NC: The Sylva Herald.
Heinrich, Bernd. 1997. *The Trees in My Forest*. NY: Cliff Street Books.

Hill, Sarah H. 1997. *Weaving New Worlds: Southeastern Cherokee Women and Their Basketry*. Chapel Hill: University of North Carolina Press.

Horton, J. Wright, Jr., and Victor A. Zullo, eds. 1991. *The Geology of the Carolinas*. Knoxville: University of Tennessee Press.

Horton, Jim. 1979. *The Summer Times*. Tampa, FL: The Cider Press, Inc.

Houk, Rose. 1993. *Great Smoky Mountains National Park: A Natural History Guide*. Boston, MA: Houghton Mifflin Company.

Hudson, Charles. 1976. *The Southeastern Indians*. Knoxville: University of Tennessee Press.

———. 1978. "Uktena: A Cherokee Anomalous Monster." *Journal of Cherokee Studies* 3 (Spring).

Hunt, Charles B. 1974. *Natural Regions of the United States and Canada*. San Francisco: W.H. Freeman and Company.

Hutchins, Ross E. 1971. *Hidden Valley of the Smokies: With a Naturalist in the Great Smoky Mountains*. New York: Dodd, Mead & Company.

Jones, Rhonda. 2004. "Will Walker—Legend of Tuckaleechee Cove." http://www.angelfire.com/tn/digginroots/wwalkdeath.html.

Kemp, Steve, ed. 1993. *Trees & Familiar Shrubs of the Smokies*. Gatlinburg, TN: Great Smoky Mountains Natural History Association.

———. 2004. *Trees & Forests—Great Smoky Mountains National Park*. Gatlinburg, TN: Great Smoky Mountains Association and the National Park Service.

Kilpatrick, Alan. 1997. *The Night Has a Naked Soul: Witchcraft and Sorcery among the Western Cherokee*. Syracuse, NY: Syracuse University Press.

Kircher, John C. 1988. *A Field Guide to the Eastern Forests—North America*. Boston: Houghton Mifflin Co.

Linzey, Donald W. 1995. *Mammals of Great Smoky Mountains National Park*. Blacksburg, VA: McDonald & Woodward Publishing Company.

Mankiller, Wilma. 1988. "The Chief Cooks: Traditional Cherokee Recipes By Principal Chief Wilma Mankiller." http://spiritvisioncrafts.tripod.com/id50.htm.

McClung, Marshall. 2002. "Eller Cove Days." *Graham* (Robbinsville, NC) *Star*, April. http://www.main.nc.us/graham/mcclung/Eller%20Cove%20Days.html.

McDaniel, Lynda. 1998. *Highroad Guide to the North Carolina Mountains*. Atlanta: Longstreet.

Moldenke, Harold N. 1949. *American Wildflowers*. NY: D. Van Nostrand Company, Inc.

Mooney, James. 1932. *The Swimmer Manuscript: Cherokee Sacred Formulas and Medical Prescriptions*. Revised, completed, and edited by Frans M. Olbrechts. Washington, DC: Government Printing Office. (For provenance and questions involving authorship of this text, see introduction to *James Mooney's History, Myths, and Sacred Formulas of the Cherokees*.)

———. 1992. *James Mooney's History, Myths, and Sacred Formulas of the Cherokees*. Biographical introduction by George Ellison. Asheville, NC: Historical Images. (Facsimile of 1900 edition of *Myths of the Cherokee*, Washington, DC: Government Printing Office, and 1891 edition of *The Sacred Formulas of the Cherokees*, Washington, DC: Government Printing Office.)

Moore, Harry L. 1988. *A Roadside Guide to the Geology of the Great Smoky Mountains National Park*. Knoxville: University of Tennessee Press.

———. 1994. *A Geologic Trip Across Tennessee by Interstate 40*. Knoxville: University of Tennessee Press.

Ovid. 1955. *The Metamorphoses of Ovid*. Translated with an introduction by Mary M. Innes. NY: Penguin Books.

Parkman, Francis. 1851. *History of the Conspiracy of Pontiac, and the War of the North American Tribes Against the English Colonies After the Conquest of Canada*. 2 vols. Boston: Little, Brown and Company.

Parris, John. 1957. *My Mountains, My People*. Asheville, NC: Citizen-Times Publishing Co.

———. 1967. *Mountain Bred*. Asheville, NC: Citizen-Times Publishing Company.

———. 1986. "The 'Boomer' Is Our Speediest Varmint." *Asheville Citizen-Times* November 9, 1986.

Patton, Alexander S. 1908. *Memory Days*. NY: Neale Publishing.

Peattie, Donald Culross. 1950. *A Natural History of Trees of Eastern and Central North America*. Boston: Houghton Mifflin Company.

Perdue, Theda. 1989. *The Cherokee*. NY: Chelsea House Publishers.

Pittillo, J. Dan, Robert D. Hatcher Jr., and Stanley W. Buol. 1998. "Introduction to the Environment and Vegetation of the Southern Blue Ridge Province." *Castanea* 3 (September).

———. 2006. Personal communications with the author by telephone and e-mail regarding the original height of the Appalachians.

Powell, William S. 1968. *The North Carolina Gazetteer: A Dictionary of Tar Heel Places*. Chapel Hill: University of North Carolina Press.

Predny, Mary L., and James L. Chamberlain. 2005. *Galax* (Galax urceolata): *An Annotated Bibliography*. Gen. Tech Rep. SRS-87. Asheville, NC: U.S. Department of Agriculture, Forest Service, Southern Research Station. (Available free from Communications, USDA Forest Service, Southern Research Station, PO Box 2680, Asheville, NC 28802-9903).

Redington, Robert J. 1978. *Survey of the Appalachians*. South Egremont, MA: Taconic Publishers.

Roe, Charles E. 1987. *A Directory to North Carolina's Natural Areas*. Raleigh: North Carolina Natural Heritage Foundation.

Rue, Leonard Lee, III. 1969. *The World of the Red Fox*. NY: J.B. Lippincott Company.

Sanders, Jack. 2003. *The Secret of Wildflowers: A Delightful Feast of Little-Known Facts, Folklore, and History*. Guilford, CT: The Globe Pequot Press. (Expanded edition of *Hedgemaids and Fairy Candles: The Lives and Lore of North American Wildflowers*, Camden, ME: Ragged Mountain Press, 1993.)

Santos, Carlos. 2001. "Are the Appalachians Getting Taller?" *Richmond Times-Dispatch* November 26, 2006.

Schafale, Michael P., and Alan S. Weakley. 1990. *Classification of the Natural Communities of North Carolina—Third Approximation*. Raleigh: North Carolina Heritage Program.

Shimer, John A. 1972. *Field Guide to Landforms in the United States*. NY: The Macmillan Company.

Simpson, Marcus B., Jr. 1992. *Birds of the Blue Ridge Mountains*. Chapel Hill: University of North Carolina Press.

Smith, Richard M. 1999. *Wildflowers of the Southern Mountains*. Knoxville: University of Tennessee Press.

Snyder, Lloyd H., Jr., and James G. Bruce.1986. *Field Guide to the Ferns and Other* Pteridophytes *of Georgia*. Athens: University of Georgia Press.

Spongberg, Stephen A. 1990. *A Reunion of Trees: The Discovery of Exotic Plants and Their Introduction into North American and European Landscapes*. Cambridge, MA: Harvard University Press.

Stokes, Donald W. 1989. *The Natural History of Wild Shrubs and Vines*. Chester, CT: The Globe Pequot Press.

Stupka, Arthur. 1963. *Notes on the Birds of Great Smoky Mountains National Park*. Knoxville: University of Tennessee Press.

———. 1964. *Trees, Shrubs, and Woody Vines of Great Smoky Mountains National Park*. Knoxville: University of Tennessee Press.

Summerlin, Vernon, and Cathy Summerlin. 1999. *Highroad Guide to the Tennessee Mountains*. Atlanta: Longstreet.

Tilley, Stephen G., and James E. Huheey. 2001. *Reptiles & Amphibians of the Smokies*. Gatlinburg, TN: Great Smoky Mountains Natural History Association.

Webster, William David, et al. 1985. *Mammals of the Carolinas, Virginia and Maryland*. Chapel Hill: University of North Carolina Press.

Weidensaul, Scott. 1994. *Mountains of the Heart: A Natural History of the Appalachians*. Golden, CO: Fulcrum Publishing.

Wharton, Charles H. 1978. *The Natural Environments of Georgia*. Atlanta: Geologic and Water Resources Division and Georgia Department of Natural Resources.

Whitaker, John O., Jr. 1980. *The Audubon Field Guide to North American Mammals*. NY: Alfred A. Knopf.

White, Peter, et al. 1996. *Wildflowers of the Smokies*. Gatlinburg, TN: Great Smoky Mountains Natural History Association.

Whittaker, R.H. 1973. "Vegetation of the Great Smoky Mountains." *Ecological Monographs* 26.

Wigginton, Elliott, ed. "Beekeeping." *Foxfire 2*. Garden City, NY: Anchor Books, Doubleday.

Winegar, Deane, and Garvey Winegar. 1998. *Highroad Guide to the Virginia Mountains*. Atlanta: Longstreet.

Wofford, B. Eugene. 1989. *Guide to the Vascular Plants of the Blue Ridge*. Athens: University of Georgia Press.

———, curator. University of Tennessee Herbarium. http://tenn.bio.utk.edu/vascular/vascular.html.

Zeigler, Wilbur G., and Ben S. Grosscup. 1883. *The Heart of the Alleghanies or Western North Carolina: Comprising Its Topography, History, Resources, People, Narratives, Incidents, and Pictures of Travel, Adventures in Hunting and Fishing, and Legends of Its Wilderness*. Raleigh, NC: Alfred Williams.

ABOUT THE AUTHOR AND ARTIST

George and Elizabeth Ellison moved with their children to western North Carolina in 1973. George's office is situated at Elizabeth Ellison Watercolors, a gallery-studio his wife owns and operates on the town square in Bryson City. Since 1976, they have made their home in a forty-six-acre cove surrounded on three sides by the Great Smoky Mountains National Park.

A native of Milton, North Carolina, Elizabeth is of Occaneechi Indian descent. Having exhibited and sold her artwork widely throughout the United States for more than thirty years, she also teaches week-long workshops at various institutions such as the Appalachian Center for Crafts in Smithville, Tennessee, and the North Carolina Arboretum in Asheville.

Utilizing both traditional and oriental techniques—and often employing American Indian motifs—she depicts the varied landscapes, wildflowers, animals and human inhabitants of the Blue Ridge Province. Elizabeth frequently gathers and processes native Appalachian plants to make the handmade papers she incorporates into her paintings: black willow, mulberry, cattail, papyrus, rush, iris, wisteria, yucca, raspberry, blackberry and more.

Her pen-and-ink drawings and watercolor washes have illustrated the work of her husband and other writers. Publishing venues include the *Asheville Citizen-Times*, *Blue Ridge Outdoors*, *Outdoor Traveler*, *Friends of Wildlife: The Journal of the North Carolina Wildlife Federation*, *High Vistas* and *Chinquapin: The Newsletter of the Southern Appalachian Botanical Society*. The exceptional quality and individuality of her work led to her inclusion in *Fodor's Guide to the National Parks and Seashores of the East*. She was also the watercolorist for the character "Alice" in the movie *Songcatcher*, filmed in the fall of 1999.

For additional information about Elizabeth's exhibitions and work visit www.elizabethellisonwatercolors.com.

George writes and lectures about the natural and human history of the Blue Ridge Province. His "Nature Journal" column, illustrated by Elizabeth, appears every other week in the *Asheville Citizen-Times* and his "Back Then" column appears weekly in *Smoky Mountain News*, a newsmagazine. His "Botanical Excursions" column, also illustrated by Elizabeth, is published quarterly in *Chinquapin: The Newsletter of the Southern Appalachian Botanical Society*. For many years, he has served as a field trip leader for bird, wildflower and fern identification workshops offered by the Native Plant Conference sponsored by Western Carolina University, the North Carolina Arboretum, Southwestern Community College and the Smoky Mountain Field School as administered by the University of Tennessee for the Great Smoky Mountains National Park.

George wrote biographical introductions for the reissues of two Southern Appalachian classics: Horace Kephart's *Our Southern Highlanders* (University of Tennessee Press, 1976) and James Mooney's *History, Myths and Sacred Formulas of the Cherokees* (Historical Images, 1992). The History Press published his collection of thirty-seven essays titled *Mountain Passages: Natural and Cultural History of Western North Carolina and the Great Smoky Mountains* in 2005. One of Elizabeth's paintings was featured on the book's cover. Since 1990, he has conducted a number of Elderhostel programs at various institutions about either Cherokee or pioneer settler history and culture.

For additional information about George's programs and how to contact him visit www.georgeellison.com.